CROSS**CURRENTS**
PURSUING SOCIAL JUSTICE AND INTERRELIGIOUS WORK
SINCE 1950

CrossCurrents (ISSN 0011-1953; online ISSN 1939-3881) connects the wisdom of the heart with the life of the mind and the experiences of the body. The journal is operated through its parent organization, the Association for Public Religion and Intellectual Life (APRIL), an interreligious network of academics, activists, artists, and community leaders seeking to engage the many ways religion meets the public. Contributions to the journal exist at the nexus of religion, education, the arts, and social justice. The journal is published quarterly on behalf of the Association for Public Religion and Intellectual Life by the University of North Carolina Press.

The Association for Public Religion and Intellectual Life (formerly ARIL) is a global network of leaders, scholars, and social change agents who explore religious life, engage in intellectual inquiry, and lead ethical action in the world today. Their primary objective, especially through annual summer colloquia and *CrossCurrents*, is to bring together leading voices of our time to advocate for justice and to examine global spiritual and interreligious currents in both historical and contemporary perspectives.

A membership to APRIL includes access to *CrossCurrents* starting with Volume 58, 2008, though our partners at Project MUSE, monthly newsletters, early access to summer colloquium themes, a 40% on UNC Press books, and more. For more information, including membership and subscription rates, visit www.aprilonline.org.

This reissue of *CrossCurrents* was one of four issues published in 2010 as part of Volume 60. For a current masthead visit www.aprilonline.org.

© 2010 Association for Public Religion and Intellectual Life. All rights reserved.

ISBN 978-1-4696-6676-1 (Print)

CROSSCURRENTS

EDITORIAL

142
Stephanie Mitchem

ARTICLES

144
Rethinking Yoga and the Application of Yoga in Modern Medicine
M. Alejandro Chaoul and Lorenzo Cohen

168
Meditation as Medicine: A Critique
Wakoh Shannon Hickey

185
The Buddhist Health Study: Meditation on Love and Compassion as Features of Religious Practice
Bruce M. Sullivan, Bill Wiist, and Heidi Wayment

208
Religion and HIV/AIDS Prevention in Nigeria
Jude Aguwa

224
Ecology and Traditional Chinese Medicine in California
Emily Wu

238
Hip-Hop Percussion and Cubist Vision: "Africa" Climbing the Spine Like an Unwanted Mime at the Post-colonial Crossroads
Jim Perkinson

257
Michael Harrington and the "Left Wing of the Possible"
Gary Dorrien

POETRY

283
Inner Light
Mariaina Kreinin

285
Walkabout
Mariaina Kreinin

286
Notes on Contributors

On the Cover: The photograph on the cover is by Goldmund Lukic who runs photo studios in Bangkok and Buenos Aires. His website is http://www.goldmundphoto.com. The photograph is © Goldmund Lukic and is used here by permission.

EDITORIAL

Stephanie Mitchem

When I was developing the ideas for my dissertation some years ago, I wanted to consider black women's religious lives in ways that had not been done before. I knew that there were some distinctive aspects, but what were they? I began to look into the connections between healing and religion because they were routes to think about black women's religious lives concretely. Our prayer lives and our bodies are not discrete, unrelated categories. We have embodied spirituality. This spirituality shapes our decisions when faced with a health crisis or what to eat, when determining our love lives and how we pray.

I've been fortunate to meet some of the leaders in this field, particularly medical anthropologist Linda Barnes. In her work at Boston University, Dr. Barnes has led many graduate students in the exploration of religion and healing. Some of the results can be seen on the web page of the Boston Healing Landscape Project, at http://www.bu.edu/bhlp. I mention Linda and her work here because she influenced my continued exploration of these ideas. I admit, though, that I regularly called her "evil" because she kept pushing me to consider "just one more" thing in my research.

I tell these research stories because religion and healing is a relatively new and definitely developing field that reflects the reality of how we live. We can understand religion as a bigger category than any particular denomination's boundaries. We can think of spirituality as a way of being in the world. Therefore, we human beings seek healing that is consonant with our religion for all aspects of our lives, from the physical to the financial to the social. It simply makes sense: Religions have concrete expressions that accompany ideas. Our spiritual lives reflect cultures as well as creeds. Researchers then explore new questions and new aspects of the dynamic interactions between religions and healing. We may ask why this group prays this way or stands in that position? We may consider when a religious practice, say, circumcision of males or females, is less religious and more bodily violation?

Health and healing practices are more than what we choose to do for a cold or childbirth. They reflect cultures, times, place, and space. Despite the arguments about health care legislation or health insurers in the United States, the plain fact is that we human beings still have our own practices, which often are not controlled by legislation but by spiritual beliefs.

This issue's contributors show the growing edges of this field. Whether considering scientific dimensions, particular religious traditions, or social injustices, these authors explore religion and healing in rich and diverse ways.

In addition, we conclude with two articles on different, but interrelated topics. Jim Perkinson pulls together two stands of artistic expression that most people would not recognize as being related, namely Hip-hop and Cubism. He makes the connections all the more vivid by using a style of writing appropriate to his topic. Perkinson writes as both a fan and a keen observer of these two art forms, as does Gary Dorrien, whose vivid portrait of Michael Harrington is sure to entertain even as it informs ... and possibly even inspires. With these, and the two poems with which this issue concludes, it should become clear that when the connections between religion and health are fully explored and acted upon, entire cultures and societies may be made whole.

RETHINKING YOGA AND THE APPLICATION OF YOGA IN MODERN MEDICINE

M. Alejandro Chaoul and Lorenzo Cohen

Yoga is a Sanskrit word that means union, to yoke, or to join; the merging of the microcosm of our existence in our body with the macrocosm. In the West, yoga is often referred to as a mind-body technique from Asia, usually categorized as meditation (for those seated practices) and yoga (practices that include movement and the active participation of the body). Therefore, "yoga" can be said to be an overarching category that includes all Asian mind-body practices, whether from India (Hatha yoga, etc.), Tibet (*Tsa lung Trul khor* [rTsa rlung 'Phrul 'khor]), China (*T'ai chi, qi gong*) or other Asian origin. In the field of complementary and alternative medicine (CAM), yogic practices can be categorized as both "energy medicine" and "mind-body medicine."[1] They can be considered "energy medicine" as they purportedly work with the subtle energies of the body. In the Tibetan tradition, for example, the category of energy (*tsel* [rtsal]) helps understand the link of mind-body, as mind-energy-body. Energy is usually manifested as breath and/or sound. The aspect of subtle breath or energy-breath is a crucial aspect of all these Asian practices. In China this *energy* is called *qi*, in India *prana*, in Tibet *lung* (*rlung*), and although each of these traditions have their own distinct mind-energy-body practices (*T'ai chi* or *qi gong* in China, Hatha Yoga in India, and *Tsa lung Trul khor* in Tibet) they all do emphasize that aspect of energy-breath or breath-energy. Scientific research has also shown that these practices modulate brain activity and diminish the psychological and biological effects of stress. As such, they are also considered in the category of "mind-body medicine." In the West, the scientific community is more comfortable considering these practices within the area of mind-body medicine, as there is still insufficient evidence to support the realm of "energy medicine."

In this article we will discuss the use of the term yoga to describe these pan-Asian mind-body practices, provide an overview of the medical research being conducted with these practices, describe our research studies, and highlight challenges and future ideas on how this interesting field can further develop within the scientific community and be better integrated with conventional medical care.

Yoga: a pan-Asian mind-body practice

There are pros and cons to using the term "yoga" to describe these Asian practices. As any individual label, the term yoga can be an overgeneralization as well as an oversimplification for categorizing different practices and traditions and may dismiss some of the uniqueness of each. However, as we add a qualifier that represents origin or style (e.g., Tibetan yoga, Hatha yoga, Kundalini yoga, etc.), by utlizing the unifying term "yoga," we can use the same category and still acknowledge the similarities and differences. It is not dissimilar from the overarching category of meditation. Most seem to agree on the use of the term "meditation," yet it comes from different traditions with some differences in the practices. The qualifiers added along with the term meditation bring forth the uniqueness of each practice but under the broad category of "meditation" (e.g., Transcendental meditation [TM], mindfulness or vipassana meditation, Zen meditation, etc.).

Although the term "yoga" is of Indian origin from Sanskrit, its use has been incorporated into the English language and adopted to encompass a large range of practices from various other traditions, including mind-body practices of Tibet and China (see, for example, the description of "Taoist yoga" by Paper and Thompson 1998).[2] As the famous religious historian and author of *Yoga: Immortality and Freedom*, Mircea Eliade, states:

> side by side with this 'classic' Yoga, there are countless forms of 'popular,' non-systematic yoga; there are also non-Brahmanic yogas (Buddhist, Jainist); above all, there are yogas whose structures are 'magical,' 'mystical,' and so on. (Eliade 1958)

Indologist David White asserts that the meditative techniques under the large rubric of yoga, as well as the Ayurveda medical system, arose as part of the interactions of the Vedic matrix with Brahmanic and Buddhist philosophical and mystical traditions. (White 1996). White adds that "[t]he organizing principles of the sixth-century BC[E] teachings of the Buddha on suffering and its cessation were essentially medical" (White 1996). Stating that, for yogins and alchemists, "the human self is an exact replica of the macrocosm," White writes that yogic practices treat the imbalances and diseases "between the bodily microcosm and the universal macrocosm." (White 1996). This is an appealing argument for the way these practices have migrated into the medical field, or in anthropologist Joseph Alter's words, the "medicalization" of yoga (Alter 2004).

White affirms that the Upanishads of the fourth and third century BCE began "charting the yogic body" and that the practice of yoga is done to achieve experiences beyond the reasoning mind. (White 1996). In the Tibetan Yogas (*Tsa lung Trul khor*), for example, the releasing of physical, energetic, and mental disease and obstacles allows the vital breath currents to flow better throughout and nurture the organism at all three levels: body, energy, and mind.

It is clear that these yogic practices are not seen as mere exercise or performance, like gymnastics and aerobics are seen in the West. In effect, Eliade asserts that, from the post-Vedic period, yoga was defined as "the means of attaining being, the effectual techniques for gaining liberation" (Eliade 1958).

With the inception of the tantric movement, which began around the fourth century BCE, and reached its apogee in India and Tibet in the eighth century, the body takes primary importance, with the specific esoteric goal of attaining liberation or "enlightenment" by means of enabling vital breath currents to flow and unblock obstacles or interruptions to that enlightenment. It is also important to note that, for the Tibetan and many of the Chinese and Indian spiritual practices known as "Mahayana" or Great Vehicle, part of the goal of the practices is that the enlightenment is not just for the practitioner, but extends to liberate all sentient beings.

On the origins or roots of tantra, White writes:

> Indian tantrism, in its Hindu, Buddhist and Jain varieties, did not emerge out of a void. It was on the one hand influenced by cultural interactions with China, Tibet, central Asia, Persia, and Europe, interactions which had the Silk Road and medieval maritime roués and ports as their venue. Much more important, however, were the indigenous Indian roots of tantrism, which was not so much a departure from earlier forms of Hinduism as their continuation, albeit in sometimes tangential and heterodox ways. (White 1996)

Tantra, as Eliade remarks, was a pan-Asian movement influenced by the local religious tradition and culture, as well as by Persia and Europe (mostly Greece) through the trade routes.

Yoga becomes one of the most evident examples in which the yogi makes the body the locus and tool for the liberation of itself. This is consistent with philosopher John Dillon, although focusing on Platonic thought, refining versus rejecting the body, which can be said to exist across cultures and traditions (Dillon 1998).

The concept of rejecting being predominant in ascetic practices and refining presented as the "Perfecting the body," "the body as a temple," and even the "immortality" of the inner or subtle body that are seen as part of the know-how of enlightenment (Eliade 1958). This understanding of the body as a tool to refine the self is more in line with the way mind and body are related both in yogic practices and in mind-body medicine.

The mind-body connection

The belief that what we think and feel can influence our health and healing dates back thousands of years (Shankar and Liao). As we have seen, the importance of the role of the mind, emotions, and behaviors in health and well being was part of traditional Chinese, Tibetan, and Ayurvedic medicine and other medical traditions of the world. Many people are now turning to these ancient practices as a way to reduce stress as there is now substantial evidence showing the negative health consequences of sustained stress on health and well being through profound psychological, behavioral, and physiological effects. These psychological and behavioral effects of stress may include increased negative effect, post-traumatic stress disorder, increased health-impairing behaviors (e.g., poor diet, lack of exercise, or substance abuse), poor sleep, and decreased quality of life, or QOL (Baum and Singer 1987). Research has shown that stress can also decrease compliance with health-screening behaviors.

Stress-induced physiological changes that can have a direct effect on health include persistent increases in sympathetic nervous system activity and the hypothalamic-pituitary-axis that can cause increased blood pressure, heart rate, catecholamine secretion, and platelet aggregation (Glaser 2005). Further, recent research suggests that stress is associated with increased latent viral reactivation, upper respiratory tract infections, and wound-healing time (Glaser and Kiecolt-Glaser 1998, 2005). Stress also deregulates a variety of immune indices, as has been found in both healthy subjects and people with cancer (Glaser and Kiecolt-Glaser 2005). Such stress-induced physiological changes may affect cancer progression, treatment, recovery, recurrence, and survival (Antoni et al. 2006, Glaser and Kiecolt-Glaser 2005). For example, several studies have linked stress and other psychosocial factors to the incidence and progression of cancer (Gehde and Balthrusch 1990, Greer et al. 1979, Morris et al. 1981). In addition, research has shown that depression, which is a common psychological response to stressful life events or circumstances, is linked to an increased risk of cancer, progression of disease, and decreased survival (Loberiza et al. 2002, Penninx et al. 1998, Steel et al. 2007, Strommel et al. 2002, Watson et al. 1999). Extensive research has also now established that stress and depression cause the suppression of cell-mediated immunity (Irwin et al. 1990, Rabin 1999). Studies in cancer patients have linked immune function, including NK cell function and T-lymphocyte proliferation, to prognosis, recurrence, and survival time. Recent laboratory research has also linked stress directly to changes in the tumor micro-environment and stress was found to be directly responsible for progression of disease and survival (Thaker et al. 2006). The clinical significance of stress-related immune and endocrine system changes and changes in the tumor micro-environment has not been widely studied. However, these changes may be significant enough to affect not only the immediate health of the patient, but also the course of the disease and thus the future health of the patient (Bovbjerg 1991, Fife et al. 1996, Glaser and Kiecolt-Glaser 2005, Redd et al. 1991, Van der Pompe et al. 1994). Decreasing distress and maintaining the functional integrity of the immune system and other physiological systems are therefore important in helping people remain healthy. Although this area of research is relatively new, it has been demonstrated that psychological factors can result in behavioral and regulatory system changes that, in turn, may affect future health (Antoni et al. 2006, Glaser and Kiecolt-Glaser 2005). This has helped to legitimize what is called the mind-body connection and mind-body medicine research.

Thus, the mind-body connection is an important aspect of integrative oncology as emphasized in the recent Institute of Medicine (IOM) report *"Cancer Care for the Whole Patient"* (IOM, 2008). In this comprehensive report it is mentioned that *"cancer care today often provides state-of-the-science biomedical treatment, but fails to address the psychological and social (psychosocial) problems associated with the illness. These problems—including... anxiety, depression or other emotional problems...—cause additional suffering, weaken adherence to prescribed treatments, and threaten patients' return to health."* Extensive research has documented that mind-body interventions appear to address many of the issues mentioned in the IOM report. Some techniques will be discussed below.

Mind-body practices

Mind-body practices are defined as a variety of techniques designed to enhance the mind's capacity to affect bodily function and symptoms (National Center for Complementary/Alternative Medicine 2008). Mind-body techniques include relaxation, hypnosis, visual imagery, meditation, biofeedback, cognitive-behavioral therapies, group support, autogenic training, and expressive arts therapies such as art, music, or dance. As mentioned earlier, therapies such as yoga (including T'ai chi, qi gong, Tsa lung, and Trul khor) often fall into the CAM category of energy medicine, as they are intended to work with bodily "energetic fields" (e.g., meridians and *qi* (pronounced chee—China), *lung* (pronounced loong—Tibet), *prana* (India), and *ki* (pronounced kee—Japan). However, they are also likely to exert strong effects through a mind-body connection and as such fall into the mind-body medicine category. Interestingly, when we examine the Asian philosophical origins of these practices, noted above, with humans viewed as a mind-energy-body system, it makes sense to combine the categories of mind-body medicine and energy medicine.

In the West, pioneering research in mind-body medicine conducted by (Benson et al. (1974a), Jon Kabat-Zinn 1982) helped to form the scientific field. Early research by (Benson et al. (1974b), Wallace et al. 1971) found that the practice of TM resulted in lowered blood pressure, reduction in oxygen consumption, heart rate, and metabolic rate, greater than is expected during sleep; with an increase in alpha waves. All these changes indicated a state of relaxation where there was diminished sympathetic nervous system activity following meditation. Benson coined the term the "relaxation response."

Benson and colleagues (Benson et al. 1982) subsequently investigated three advanced practitioners of the Tibetan meditative practice called *tum-mo,* who were living in the lower Himalayas. Practitioners of *tum-mo* claim to increase their body temperature through a special meditative technique of deep concentration. Traditionally, these practices are done in a very cold environment with minimal clothes on the practitioners' body to see if they could dry a wet sheet at under 40°F and then wet the dry sheet by the perspiration of their body as they continued performing the *tum-mo* practice. In the cold environment the advanced *tum-mo* practitioners could increase the temperature of their fingers and toes by as much as 8.3°C (Benson et al. 1982). A significant reduction in their oxygen consumption was also observed.

Kabat-Zinn developed a combination of *Vipassana* (a Buddhist mindfulness meditation technique), some yoga postures, and a body scan technique in a behavioral medicine setting for populations with various types of chronic pain (J. Kabat-Zinn 1990, Kabat-Zinn et al. 1985). Originally called Stress Reduction and Relaxation Program (SR-RP), and later coined as Mindfulness-based Stress Reduction (MBSR), it was described as "paying attention in a particular way: on purpose, in the present moment, and nonjudgementally" (J. Kabat-Zinn 1990). MBSR has been extensively scientifically investigated in the West and is useful for helping to ease psychological and physical effects of some chronic illnesses and produces changes in brain activity and biological processes (Davidson et al. 2003, Grossman et al. 2004, Ott et al. 2006). Today, practices that fall into the category of mind-body medicine are no longer considered "alternative" and they are well integrated into conventional medicine and most medical settings (e.g., hypnosis, biofeedback, cognitive-behavioral therapy, and group support). As research continues, the treatments that are found beneficial will hopefully become integrated into conventional medical care.

Mind-body practices in cancer

Research has shown that after being diagnosed with cancer, patients try to bring about positive changes in their lifestyles, often seeking to take control of their health (Blanchard et al. 2003). Techniques of stress management that have proven helpful include progressive muscle relaxation (Baider et al. 1994, Sloman 1995), diaphragmatic breathing (Moskowitz 1996, Ross et al. 1999), guided imagery (Spiegel 1997, Walker et al. 1999, K. G. Wallace 1997), social support (M. A. Richardson et al. 1997, Turner-Cobb et al. 2000), and meditation (Coker 1999, Massion et al. 1995). Participating in stress management programs prior to treatment have enabled patients to tolerate therapy with fewer reported side effects (Arakawa 1997, Manyande et al. 1995, Syrjala and Chapko 1995, Troesch et al. 1993). Supportive expressive group therapy has also been found to be useful for patients with cancer (Fawzy et al. 1995, Helgeson et al. 2000, Spiegel et al. 1981). Psychosocial interventions have been shown to specifically decrease depression and anxiety and to increase self-esteem and active-approach coping strategies (Fawzy et al. 1990, Gordon 2008, Helgeson et al. 1999, Richardson et al. 1990).

A meta-analysis of 116 studies found that mind-body therapies could reduce anxiety, depression and mood disturbance in cancer patients, and assist their coping skills (Devine and Westlake 1995). Newell and colleagues (Newell et al. 2002) reviewed psychological therapies for cancer patients and concluded that interventions involving self-practice and hypnosis for managing nausea and vomiting could be recommended, but that further research was suggested to examine the benefits of relaxation training and guided imagery. Further research was also warranted to examine the benefits of relaxation and guided imagery for managing general nausea, anxiety, quality of life, and overall physical symptoms (Newell et al. 2002). More recently, Ernst et al. (2007) examined the change in the state of the evidence for mind-body therapies for various medical conditions between 2000 and 2005 and found that there is now maximal evidence for the use of relaxation techniques for anxiety, hypertension, insomnia, and nausea due to chemotherapy.

Research examining meditation and yoga practices incorporated into cancer care suggests that these mind-body practices help to improve aspects of quality of life including improved mood, sleep quality, physical functioning, and overall well being (Bower et al. 2005, Gordon 2008). Hypnosis, and especially self-hypnosis, has been found to be beneficial to help reduce distress and discomfort during difficult medical procedures (Spiegel and Moore 1997). An NIH Technology Assessment Panel found strong evidence for hypnosis in alleviating cancer-related pain (1996). Hypnosis effectively treats anticipatory nausea in pediatric (Zeltzer et al. 1991) and adult cancer patients (Morrow and Morrell 1982), reduces post-operative nausea and vomiting (Faymonville et al. 1997), and improves adjustment to invasive medical procedures (Lang et al. 2000, 2006, Montgomery et al. 2007).

Mind-body practice at the University of Texas M. D. Anderson cancer center
Ten years ago, with the advise of Tenzin Wangyal Rinpoche of the Ligmincha Institute, we began a Tibetan meditation class at The University of Texas M. D. Anderson Cancer Center's Place... *of wellness* in Houston, Texas. Place... *of wellness* is M. D. Anderson's clinical delivery center for complementary and integrative medicine. The program was called *Connecting with Your Heart*, a technique to help cancer patients and their families calm their minds and use their breath to connect to their inner *home*.

For more than ten years, we have also been conducting scientific research on the possible benefits of these yoga practices in people with cancer. Our research simultaneously examines the behavioral, physiological, psychological, and spiritual outcomes of these practices in different cancer populations at different points in their cancer journey. There are a number of ongoing studies funded by the National Cancer Institute (NCI), The National Institutes of Health, investigating the effects of yoga (from the Indian tradition—Patanjali-based practices; Tibetan tradition—Tsa Lung, Trul Khor; and Chinese tradition–qi gong/T'ai chi).

Two initial studies conducted by our group examined the effects of Tsa lung and Trul khor. For these pilot studies, a seven-session program called "Tibetan Yoga" (TY) was designed, and included practices from the Tibetan Bon tradition, included in the Mother Tantra *(Ma rgyud)* and Great Completeness Oral Transmission of Zhang Zhung *(Zhang zhung snyan rgyud)*. The intervention, chosen in consultation with Tenzin

Wangyal Rinpoche, consisted of four main components: (1) breathing exercises, (2) meditative concentration, (3) *tsa-lung* sitting yogic postures, and (4) *trul-khor* yogic postures involving more physical movement. These components have been used in the Bon tradition for centuries and we chose them with the intention that they would help in ameliorating side-effects and hastening recovery for patients who were either undergoing active treatment or who had recently completed treatment.

The breathing exercises help participants to regulate their breath and prepare for the movement-based practice. The breathing techniques are thought to help calm the mind and manage physical, emotional, and mental "obstacles." The meditative concentration techniques the patients learned helped them to use the calmness of the mind towards self-observation and to guide the breath to clear away obstacles. They also learned a simple meditative technique that incorporated sound and visualization. The *tsa lung* exercises applied the meditative concentration techniques and the breathing exercises already learned with five specific simple movements focused in different areas of the body at points called *chakras* (located at the head, neck, chest, lower abdomen, and perineum), to help participants relax and feel invigorated. The first five movements from the *trul khor* were then introduced and again the participants used the meditative concentration techniques and the breathing exercises while performing the simple movements. All the techniques were done either sitting on a cushion on the floor or sitting in a chair. The classes were taught by an instructor authorized by the Ligmincha Institute. The hour long classes were taught once a week for seven weeks. This provided the participants the opportunity to learn the techniques and practice them with the instructor, so that they could continue to practice them on their own. At the end of each class, the participants received printed material to take home and use as support of the techniques learned in that session. At the end of the course, the participants were given an audiotape with guided practices of all the techniques they learned. Participants were advised to continue daily practice at home in addition to the class at the clinic and also to continue their practice after the seven-week course was over. Patients completed measures of intrusive thoughts and avoidance behaviors, depressive symptoms, sleep disturbances, fatigue, and quality of life at baseline, one week, and one and three months after the last class.

In the first pilot study we examined the feasibility, acceptability, and initial efficacy of the TY program described above for patients with lymphoma. Patients had to be currently undergoing treatment or had to have completed treatment within the past twelve months. Thirty-nine patients were randomly assigned to either the TY group or to a waitlisted control group. The intervention group received the seven-week TY program and the wait list control group could receive the instruction after the end of the study.

Overall, the results indicated that the TY program was feasible and well liked by the patients. The majority of participants indicated that the program was "a little" or "definitely" beneficial, with no one indicating "not beneficial," and they continued practicing at least once a week, with many continuing to practice twice a week or more (Cohen et al. 2004). The study results indicated that the TY group reported lower overall sleep disturbances during the follow-up period than did the control group, with better overall sleep quality, less difficulty falling asleep, slept significantly longer, and used fewer sleep medications. Improving sleep quality in a cancer population may be particularly salient as sleep is crucial for recovery. Fatigue and sleep disturbances are common problems for patients with cancer.

A second study examined the benefits of the same seven-week TY program for women with breast cancer. Women with stage I–III breast cancer who were undergoing active treatment (radiotherapy or chemotherapy) or who underwent treatment less than one year prior to enrollment were recruited to participate in the study. Fifty-nine women were randomized to either the yoga group or a wait list control group. Initial analyses have been conducted and presented at national meetings (Cohen et al. 2005). On average, the participants in the TY group said they found the program useful or very useful, and they practiced it around twice a week. Results indicated that the yoga group reported lower cancer-related intrusive thoughts scores than the control group by the three-month assessment. They also reported lower scores for cancer-related symptoms at the one-week follow-up than the control group.

These pilot studies are among the few studies of yoga in a cancer patient population and the only scientific studies of TY in any population. We are now conducting a large NCI-funded trial examining the effects of TY for women with breast cancer undergoing chemotherapy.

Women in the TY group are being compared to women who learn some simple stretching exercises and to women in a wait list control group.

A subsequent randomized pilot trial examined the effects of yoga from the Indian tradition (Vivekananda yoga from the Patanjali yoga tradition). This was a collaborated study between the M. D. Anderson and the Vivekananda Yoga Anusandhana Samsthana (VYASA), a yoga research foundation and University in Bengaluru, India with extensive clinical and research experience conducting this form of yoga with healthy and medical populations (Nagarathna and Nagendra 1985, Nagendra and Nagarathna 1986a,b). Sixty-one women with breast cancer undergoing radiation treatment were either assigned to the yoga group or a wait-list control group that could participate in the yoga after the study was completed. Patients in the yoga group participated in the yoga sessions twice a week for the duration of their radiotherapy, each session lasting about one hour. The yoga program consisted of four main components: (1) various loosening exercises; (2) seven simple postures and a deep relaxation technique; (3) alternate nostril breathing; and (4) meditation. The components were specifically designed and selected for use in patients with cancer, with particular emphasis on the problems that women experience while undergoing radiotherapy for breast cancer and recovering from surgery and/or chemotherapy. The overall aim of these techniques was to train the participants to regulate their breathing, be aware of the various changes that occur in the body while performing the maneuvers, and by doing so the participants can calm the mind and relax parts of the body. In the beginning, patients were introduced to each of the four different areas over a period of four one-hour classes conducted by a VYASA certified Instructor. During the remainder of the sessions, the participants practiced the complete program. The exercises were done to meet each patient's needs. At the end of each of the first four classes, the participants were given a CD with a recording of the technique they just learned and some printed materials that they could take home. After the fourth session, they were given a CD with all instructions as well as a complete printed version. Participants were advised to continue daily practice at home in addition to the class at the hospital and also after the completion of radiotherapy.

The loosening and breathing exercises consisted of various gentle, sometimes repetitive, movements of the arms, legs, neck, and eyes in standing, sitting, and supine positions. Postures, or *asanas*, were done standing, sitting, or lying down (either face down or face up). These postures consisted of simple movements that included a side bending posture, two forward bending postures, three back bending postures, and a partial shoulder stand with wall support. The session always ended with the supine relaxation posture to allow the body to relax completely. In this position, they practiced the deep relaxation technique that incorporated gentle sounds that would resonate their body (e.g., "aah", "uuu", "mmm", "om"). Alternate nostril breathing was done for five rounds, sitting with the back and neck straight. Meditation was done sitting in any comfortable position or sitting on a chair. The patients were instructed to close their eyes, and concentrate on their breath and their thoughts. They were then encouraged to repeat the syllable "mmm" mentally. They were instructed to sit in silence and dwell on a single positive thought of their choice. This could be continued for about ten to twenty minutes.

Patients completed measures at baseline, one week, and one and three months after the last radiation therapy. The results indicated significantly better general health perception and physical functioning scores one-week post-radiotherapy, higher levels of cancer-related intrusive thoughts one-month post-radiotherapy, and greater finding meaning (ability to find meaning in the cancer experience) three-months post-radiotherapy (Chandwani et al., 2010). Due to the unexpected group differences in intrusive thoughts one-month post-radiotherapy, with the yoga reporting significantly greater scores than the control group, we explored the association between intrusive thoughts one month post-radiotherapy and finding meaning three months post-radiotherapy. There was a significant positive correlation between intrusive thoughts one month post-radiotherapy and finding meaning three months post-radiotherapy, suggesting that the higher the level of intrusive thoughts the greater the finding meaning at three months post-radiotherapy. Although the increase in intrusive thoughts was not expected, it does fit a model for contemplative-based mind-body practices. Within the yoga program, similar to mindfulness practices, participants are told to not avoid negative thoughts, but to simply observe them in a non-judgmental manner. This could lead to the increased frequency of intrusive thoughts, but the intrusive thoughts do not result in negative outcomes and, in fact, help with processing of the cancer experience. Comments from individual patients also indicated high acceptance of the program. A similar study funded by the NCI was recently completed where the participants were randomized to one of three groups—a yoga group, stretching group, or a wait list control group. In this study we are examining the biobehavioral effects of the yoga program using a more appropriate control group in order to separate the effects of yoga from social support and simple stretching exercises. The initial analyses suggest similar outcomes as the previous study, with the yoga group having the best outcomes followed by the stretching group. We will now be conducting a much larger trial funded by the NCI with 600 women with breast cancer undergoing radiotherapy to definitely show the benefits of incorporating yoga into the treatment plan and in addition to the standard assessments we will be examining cost-effectiveness analysis, work and/or home productivity, and health care utilization.

A mindfulness relaxation study headed by Dr. Jon Hunter from Mount Sinai Hospital, Toronto, Canada, is being conducted within the M. D. Anderson Community Clinical Oncology Program (CCOP). The purpose of the study is to test this relaxation intervention in reducing psychological and physiological side effects of chemotherapy in cancer patients. In this randomized trial, patients with newly diagnosed cancer who are about to undergo chemotherapy are randomly assigned to one of three groups: the mindfulness relaxation group (MR), a relaxing music group (RM) where participants listen to relaxing music for the same amount of time as the MR participants, or a standard care control group (SC) where participants receive standard medical education on chemotherapy. Patients complete assessments before being randomized (baseline), in the middle of their course of chemotherapy, at the end of treatment, and three months after the end of treatment. They also complete very brief diary assessments for three days before the start of each cycle of chemotherapy and for three days after. Blood samples for immune indices are also being obtained.

The mindfulness relaxation intervention consists of a script containing elements of relaxation induction, yoga breathing, guided imagery, and a "mindful" attitude, which encourages people to become aware and take notice of physical sensations without having to alter or respond to them (J. Kabat-Zinn et al. 1985). Nurses at each site are trained in the administration of the script, and subsequently deliver it to patients before their first chemotherapy session, in order to establish a pre-emptive association between relaxation and the chemotherapy setting, that will in turn diminish the development of conditioned symptoms. The patients are also given a CD of the MR recorded by the site nurse who delivered the MR training to use at home for practice sessions, and for all chemotherapy sessions.

Each time the patient attends a chemotherapy session the MR exercise is conducted prior to and during chemotherapy delivery, via use of a portable CD player with the recorded version. Participants are instructed to use the CD at home at least once daily throughout chemotherapy delivery in order to become familiar with and build skill in the technique. The participants in the RM group use a CD with relaxing music. Patients in the RM group utilize their CD in a manner identical to the MR CD, but they do not receive any specific instructions on relaxation or meditation. They also receive general information on the management of symptoms related to chemotherapy in a session of equivalent time to the MR training session. The SC arm receives general information on the management of symptoms related to chemotherapy in the manner that is typical of that CCOP site. The single arm feasibility pilot trial went well and the large phase III randomized trial is now underway (N = 300; 100 patients in each group).

We are also examining the feasibility and initial efficacy of implementing a Tibetan Sound Meditation program for women who have undergone chemotherapy for breast cancer and report cognitive deficits. There is evidence to suggest that meditation would be especially useful for this common side effect of chemotherapy (Biegler et al. 2009). The women are randomized to a meditation group or a wait-list control group. Participants in the meditation group attend two meditation sessions each week for six weeks. Standardized objective tests assessing higher order cognitive function and self-report measures of fatigue, quality of life, mental health, and sleep disturbances are administered one week prior to starting the meditation intervention. The self-report measures are then administered during the middle and final week of the intervention and 1 month after the meditation intervention ends. The standardized cognitive assessments are administered again 1 month after the meditation intervention ends. We predict that scores assessing cognitive function for women receiving the intervention will improve from baseline to post-intervention assessments and the women in the control group are expected to stay the same. Women in the intervention group will also report fewer or less severe side effects and better QOL than women in the control group.

A recently completed pilot project examined the effects of qi gong for patients with breast cancer undergoing radiotherapy. This study was conducted at the Fudan University Cancer Hospital, Shanghai, China as part of an International Center of Traditional Chinese Medicine for Cancer funded by the NCI. Patients with breast cancer who are undergoing radiotherapy were randomly assigned to either a qi gong group or a wait-list control group. Participants in the qi gong group attend daily qi gong sessions five days/week throughout their six-week radiotherapy schedule. The sessions were coordinated with the treatment schedule. The patients were taught a modified version *Gualin Qi Gong* including preparation exercises (standing posture, breathing exercise, and opening and closing of the *dantian* (an important focus point for internal meditative techniques, located in the abdomen three finger widths below and two finger-widths behind the navel), main exercise (slow exercise and fast exercise), and then the closing exercise. The focus is on working with gentle movements and breath to help regulate the patients' *qi*. Measures were obtained prior to randomization, mid-way through radiotherapy, during last week of radiotherapy, and one and three months after the end of radiotherapy.

A similar trial, funded by the NCI, is being conducted at M. D. Anderson where we are examining incorporating qi gong and T'ai chi into the treatment plan for patients with anal, rectal, or prostate cancer during radiotherapy. The program consists of several breathing and moving exercises, along with a short eight-form T'ai chi set. The overall aim of these techniques is to train the participants to regulate their breathing and become aware of the various changes that occur within their body while performing the various forms. By doing so, the participants will learn to easily calm the mind after stimulation; relax various parts of the body and the mind; and revitalize their *qi*. Patients in the comparison groups either participate in a light exercise program or receive the standard of care. Similar to our other studies, measures are obtained prior to randomization, mid-way through radiotherapy, during last week of radiotherapy, and one and three months after the end of radiotherapy.

Conclusions

For thousands of years, many cultures of the world have been examining yoga and how it leads to better understanding human existence. This *experimentation* has mainly been through introspection and the first person narrative. It is only within the past few decades that Western science has begun to seriously examine these yogic practices to determine how they affect psychological, behavioral, physiological, and biological processes. It is clear that at minimum these practices result in an acute relaxation response, lowering blood pressure, heart rate, and subjective rating of stress. More recent research is showing that these different practices can help people suffering from chronic illnesses. Each year the evidence mounts showing another medical population that is helped with the incorporation of these practices alongside conventional Western medical care.

The big strides in our understanding of the role of mind-body practices in health and well being comes from some of the studies examining psychological, behavioral, *and* biological outcomes. Demonstrating that these yogas not only make you feel better but also have an impact on our brain activity, immune function, and endocrine function, as an example, provides a better indication for the profound implication these practices can have within a medical setting. Scientists need to push the boundaries even further and examine the clinical implications and conduct the important cost-effectiveness research to begin to understand the role of these practices to improve the health and well being of humankind. A challenge to the field has always been the limited funding available to this kind of research versus the conventional biomedical fields of study. Although the funding still remains relatively quite limited, it has increased in the past ten years and interest continues to mount. The more evidence accumulates for the role of mind-body practices in medical care the greater the allotment of funding this area will receive.

Many medical centers already have incorporated mind-body practices as part of the standard of care. Although these practices are not necessarily *prescribed* and thought of in the same way as conventional medications, they are being delivered alongside medical treatments to help improve outcomes. As more evidence accumulates, the day will come when mind-body practices are a form of medical treatment provided and prescribed as part of standard medical treatment around the world.

Works cited

Alter, Joseph, 2004, *Yoga in Modern India: The Body Between Science and Philosophy*, Princeton, NJ, and Oxford, England: Princeton University Press.

Antoni, M. H., S. K. Lutgendorf, S. W. Cole, F. S. Dhabhar, S. E. Sephton, and P. G. McDonald, 2006, "The Influence of Bio-Behavioural Factors on Tumour Biology: Pathways and Mechanisms," *Nature Reviews. Cancer* 6(3), pp. 240–8.

Arakawa, S., 1997, "Relaxation to Reduce Nausea, Vomiting, and Anxiety Induced by Chemotherapy in Japanese Patients," *Cancer Nursing* 20(5), pp. 342–9.

Baider, L., B. Uziely, and A. K. De-Nour, 1994, "Progressive Muscle Relaxation and Guided Imagery in Cancer Patients," *General Hospital Psychiatry* 16(5), pp. 340–7.

Baum, A., and J. E. Singer, 1987, *Handbook of Psychology and Health: Vol V - Stress*, Hillsdale, NJ: Erlbaum.

Benson, H., J. F. Beary, and M. P. Carol, 1974a, "The Relaxation Response," *Psychiatry* 37(1), pp. 37–46.

Benson, H., J. W. Lehmann, M. S. Malhotra, R. F. Goldman, J. Hopkins, and M. D. Epstein, 1982, "Body Temperature Changes During the Practice of g Tum-mo yoga," *Nature*, 295(5846), pp. 234–6.

Benson, H., B. A. Rosner, B. R. Marzetta, and H. M. Klemchuk, 1974b, "Decreased Blood-Pressure in Pharmacologically Treated Hypertensive Patients Who Regularly Elicited the Relaxation Response," *Lancet*, 1(7852), pp. 289–91.

Biegler, K. A., M. A. Chaoul, and L. Cohen, 2009, "Cancer, Cognitive Impairment, and Meditation," *Acta Oncologica* 48(1), pp. 18–26.

Blanchard, C. M., M. M. Denniston, F. Baker, S. R. Ainsworth, K. S. Courneya, and D. M. Hann, 2003, "Do Adults Change Their Lifestyle Behaviors After a Cancer Diagnosis?" *American Journal of Health Behavior* 27(3), pp. 246–56.

Bovbjerg, D. H., 1991, "Psychoneuroimmunology. Implications for Oncology?" *Cancer*, 67, pp. 828–32.

Bower, J. E., A. Woolery, B. Sternlieb, and D. Garet, 2005, "Yoga for Cancer Patients and Survivors," *Cancer Control* 12(3), pp. 165–71.

Chandwani, K. D., B. Thornton, G. H. Perkins, B. Arun, N. V. Raghuram, and H. R. Nagendra, 2010, "Yoga Improves Quality of Life and Benefit Finding in Women Undergoing Radiotherapy for Breast Cancer," *Journal of the Society for Integrative Oncology* 8(2), pp. 43–55.

Cohen, L., B. Thornton, G. Perkins, K. Chandwani, J. Sterner, and A. Chaoul-Reich, 2005, "A Randomized Trial of a Tibetan Yoga Intervention for Breast Cancer Patients," *Psychosomatic Medicine*, 67(1), pp. A33.

Cohen, L., C. Warneke, R. T. Fouladi, M. A. Rodriguez, and A. Chaoul-Reich, 2004, "Psychological Adjustment and Sleep Quality in a Randomized Trial of the Effects of a Tibetan Yoga Intervention in Patients with Lymphoma," *Cancer*, 100(10), pp. 2253–60.

Coker, K. H., 1999, "Meditation and Prostate Cancer: Integrating a Mind/Body Intervention with Traditional Therapies," *Seminars in Urologic Oncology*, 17(2), pp. 111–8.

Davidson, R. J., J. Kabat-Zinn, J. Schumacher, M. Rosenkranz, D. Muller, and S. F. Santorelli, 2003, "Alterations in Brain and Immune Function Produced by Mindfulness Meditation," *Psychosomatic Medicine*, 65(4), pp. 564–70.

Devine, E. C., and S. K. Westlake, 1995, "The Effects of Psychoeducational Care Provided to Adults with Cancer: Meta-Analysis of 116 Studies," *Oncology Nursing Forum*, 22(9), pp. 1369–81.

Dillon, John (1998, rp. 2002). "Rejecting and Refining the Body," in Vincent Wimbush, and Richard Valantasis, eds., *Asceticism*, pp. 80–87. New York: Oxford University Press.

Eliade, Mircea, 1958 rp.1990, *Yoga: Immortality and Freedom*, Princeton, NJ: Princeton University Press.

Ernst, E., M. H. Pittler, B. Wider, and K. Boddy, 2007, "Mind-body Therapies: Are the Trial Data Getting Stronger?" *Alternative Therapies in Health and Medicine* 13(5), pp. 62–4.

Evans-Wentz, W.Y., 1935 (rp. 1958), *Tibetan Yoga and Secret Doctrines*, London and New York: Oxford University Press.

Fawzy, F. I., N. Cousins, N. W. Fawzy, M. E. Kemeny, R. Elashoff, and D. Morton, 1990, "A Structured Psychiatric Intervention for Cancer Patients. I. Changes Over Time in Methods of Coping and Affective Disturbance," *Archives of General Psychiatry*, 47(8), pp. 720–5.

Fawzy, F. I., N. W. Fawzy, L. A. Arndt, and R. O. Pasnau, 1995, "Critical Review of Psychosocial Interventions in Cancer Care," *Archives of General Psychiatry*, 52(2), pp. 100–13.

Faymonville, M. E., P. H. Mambourg, J. Joris, B. Vrijens, J. Fissette, A. Albert and M. Lamy, 1997, "Psychological Approaches During Conscious Sedation. Hypnosis Versus Stress Reducing Strategies: A Prospective Randomized Study," *Pain*, 73(3), pp. 361–7.

Fife, A., P. J. Beasley, and D. L. Fertig, 1996, "Psychoneuroimmunology and Cancer: Historical Perspectives and Current Research," *Advances in Neuroimmunology*, 6), pp. 179–90.

Gehde, E., and H. J. F. Balthrusch, 1990, "Early Experience and Development of Cancer in Later Life: Implications for Psychoimmunologic Research," *International Journal of Neuroscience*, 51), pp. 257–60.

Glaser, R., 2005, "Stress-Associated Immune Dysregulation and Its Importance for Human Health: A Personal History of Psychoneuroimmunology," *Brain, Behavior, & Immunity*, 19(1), pp. 3–11.

Glaser, R., and J. K. Kiecolt-Glaser, 1998, "Stress-associated Immune Modulation: Relevance to Viral Infections and Chronic Fatigue Syndrome," *American Journal of Medicine*, 105(3A), pp. 35S–42S.

Glaser, R., and J. K. Kiecolt-Glaser, 2005, "Stress-induced Immune Dysfunction: Implications for Health," *Nature Reviews. Immunology*, 5(3), pp. 243–51.

Gordon, J. S., 2008, "Mind-body Medicine and Cancer," in L. Cohen, and M. Frenkel, eds, *Integrative Medicine in Oncology: Hematology/Oncology Clinics of North America* (Vol. 22), Philadelphia: W B Saunders Co-Elsevier Inc, pp. 683–708.

Greer, S., T. Morris, and K. W. Pettingale, 1979, "Psychological Response to Breast Cancer: Effect on Outcome," *Lancet*, 2, pp. 1239–48.

Grossman, P., L. Niemann, S. Schmidt, and H. Walach, 2004, "Mindfulness-based Stress Reduction and Health Benefits: A Meta-Analysis," *Journal of Psychosomatic Research*, 57(1), pp. 35–43.

Helgeson, V. S., S. Cohen, R. Schulz, and J. Yasko, 1999, "Education and Peer Discussion Group Interventions and Adjustment to Breast Cancer," *Archives of General Psychiatry*, 56(4), pp. 340–7.

Helgeson, V. S., S. Cohen, R. Schulz, and J. Yasko, 2000, "Group Support Interventions for Women with Breast Cancer: Who Benefits from What?" *Health Psychology*, 19(2), pp. 107–14.

IOM, 2008, *Institute of Medicine: Cancer Care for the Whole Patient: Meeting Psychosocial Health Needs*. The National Academies Press 2008 Prepublication available online, Washington D.C.: The National Academies Press.

Irwin, M., T. Patterson, T. L. Smith, C. Caldwell, S. A. Brown, J. C. Gillin et al., 1990, "Reduction of Immune Function in Life Stress and Depression," *Biological Psychiatry*, 27, pp. 22–30.

Kabat-Zinn, J., 1982, "An Outpatient Program in Behavioral Medicine for Chronic Pain Patients Based on the Practice of Mindfulness Meditation: Theoretical Considerations and Preliminary Results," *General Hospital Psychiatry*, 4, pp. 33–47.

Kabat-Zinn, J., 1990, *Full Catastrophe Living: Using the Wisdom of Your Body and Mind to Face Stress, Pain, and Illness*, New York: Delacourt.

Kabat-Zinn, J., L. Lipworth, and R. Burney, 1985, "The Clinical use of Mindfulness Meditation for the Self-Regulation of Chronic Pain," *Journal of Behavioral Medicine* 8(2), pp. 163–90.

Lang, E. V., E. G. Benotsch, L. J. Fick, S. Lutgendorf, M. L. Berbaum, K. S. Berbaum *et al.*, 2000, "Adjunctive Non-Pharmacological Analgesia for Invasive Medical Procedures: A Randomised Trial," *Lancet* 355(9214), pp. 1486–90.

Lang, E. V., S. Berbaum, O. Faintuch, N. Hatsiopoulou et al., 2006, "Adjunctive Self-Hypnotic Relaxation for Outpatient Medical Procedures: A Prospective Randomized Trial with Women Undergoing Large Core Breast Biopsy," *Pain* 126(1–3), pp. 155–64.

Lester, Robert C., 1973, *Theravada Buddhism in Southeast Asia*, Ann Arbor: University of Michigan Press.

Loberiza, F. R., J. D. Rizzo, C. N. Bredeson, J. H. Antin, M. M. Horowitz, J. C. Weeks et al., 2002, "Association of Depressive Syndrome and Early Deaths Among Patients After Stem-Cell Transplantation for Malignant Diseases," *Journal of Clinical Oncology* 20(8), pp. 2118–26.

Manyande, A., S. Berg, D. Gettins, S. C. Stanford, S. Mazhero, D. F. Marks et al., 1995, "Preoperative Rehearsal of Active Coping Imagery Influences Subjective and Hormonal Responses to Abdominal Surgery," *Psychosomatic Medicine*, 57(2), pp. 177–82.

Massion, A. O., J. Teas, J. R. Hebert, M. D. Wertheimer, and J. Kabat-Zinn, 1995, "Meditation, Melatonin and Breast/Prostate Cancer: Hypothesis and Preliminary Data," *Medical Hypotheses*, 44(1), pp. 39–46.

Montgomery, G. H., D. H. Bovbjerg, J. B. Schnur, D. David, A. Goldfarb, C. R. Weltz et al., 2007, "A Randomized Clinical Trial of a Brief Hypnosis Intervention to Control Side Effects in Breast Surgery Patients," *Journal of the National Cancer Institute*, 99(17), pp. 1304–12.

Morris, T., S. Greer, K. W. Pettingale, and M. Watson, 1981, "Patterns of Expression of Anger and Their Psychological Correlates in Women with Breast Cancer," *Journal of Psychosomatic Research*, 25, pp. 111–7.

Morrow, G. R., and C. Morrell, 1982, "Behavioral Treatment for the Anticipatory Nausea and Vomiting Induced by Cancer Chemotherapy," *New England Journal of Medicine*, 307(24), pp. 1476–80.

Moskowitz, L., 1996, "Psychological Management of Postsurgical Pain and Patient Adherence," *Hand Clinics*, 12(1), pp. 129–37.

Nagarathna, R., and H. R. Nagendra, 1985, "Yoga for Bronchial Asthma: A Controlled Study," *British Medical Journal (Clinical Research Ed.)*, 291(6502), pp. 1077–9.

Nagendra, H. R., and R. Nagarathna, 1986a, Applications of Integrated Approach of Yoga Therapy - A Review. A New Life for Asthmatics, Bangalore, India: Vivekananda Kendra.

Nagendra, H. R., and R. Nagarathna, 1986b, "An Integrated Approach of Yoga Therapy for Bronchial Asthma: A 3-54-month Prospective Study," *Journal of Asthma* 23(3), pp. 123–37.

National Center for Complementary/Alternative Medicine. *What Is Complementary and Alternative Medicine?* Retrieved June 24, 2008, from http://nccam.nih.gov/health/whatiscam/.

National Institutes of Health Technology Assessment Panel on Integration of Behavioral, Relaxation Approaches into the Treatment of Chronic Pain and Insomnia, 1996,

"Integration of Behavioral and Relaxation Approaches into the Treatment of Chronic Pain and Insomnia," *JAMA* 276, pp. 313–8.

Newell, S. A., R. W. Sanson-Fisher, and N. J. Savolainen, 2002, "Systematic Review of Psychological Therapies for Cancer Patients: Overview and Recommendations for Future Research," *Journal of the National Cancer Institute* 94(8), pp. 558–84.

Norbu, Namkhai, 2008, *Yantra Yoga: The Tibetan Yoga of Movement*, Ithaca, NY: SnowLion Publications.

Ott, M. J., R. L. Norris, and S. M. Bauer-Wu, 2006, "Mindfulness Meditation for Oncology Patients: A Discussion and Critical Review," *Integrative Cancer Therapies* 5(2), pp. 98–108.

Paper, Jordan, and L. Thompson, 1998, *The Chinese Way in Religion*, Belmont, CA: Wadsworth Publishing Company (I.T.P.).

Penninx, B. W., J. M. Guralnik, M. Pahor, L. Ferrucci, J. R. Cerhan, R. B. Wallace et al., 1998, "Chronically Depressed Mood and Cancer Risk in Older Persons," *Journal of the National Cancer Institute* 90, pp. 1888–93.

Rabin, B. S., 1999, *Stress, Immune Function, and Health: The Connection*, New York: Wiley-Liss & Sons.

Redd, W. H., P. M. Silberfarb, B. L. Andersen, M. A. Andrykowski, D. H. Bovbjerg, T. G. Burish et al., 1991, "Physiologic and Psychobehavioral Research in Oncology," *Cancer*, 67(3), pp. 813–22.

Richardson, J. L., D. R. Shelton, M. Krailo, and A. M. Levine, 1990, "The Effect of Compliance with Treatment on Survival Among Patients with Hematologic Malignancies," *Journal of Clinical Oncology*, 8(2), pp. 356–64.

Richardson, M. A., J. Post-White, E. A. Grimm, L. A. Moye, S. E. Singletary, and B. Justice, 1997, "Coping, Life Attitudes, and Immune Responses to Imagery and Group Support after Breast Cancer Treatment," *Alternative Therapies in Health & Medicine* 3(5), pp. 62–70.

Roach, MIchael, 2004, *The Tibetan Book of Yoga: Ancient Buddhist Teachings on the Philosophy and Practice of Yoga*, Garden City, NY: Doubleday.

Ross, M. C., A. S. Bohannon, D. C. Davis, and L. Gurchiek, 1999, "The Effects of a Short-Term Exercise Program on Movement, Pain, and Mood in the Elderly. Results of a Pilot Study," *Journal of Holistic Nursing*, 17(2), pp. 139–47.

Shankar, K., and L. P. Liao, 2004, "Traditional Systems of Medicine," *Physical Medicine & Rehabilitation Clinics of North America*, 15(4), pp. 725–47.

Sloman, R., 1995, "Relaxation and the Relief of Cancer Pain," *Nursing Clinics of North America*, 30(4), pp. 697–709.

Spiegel, D., 1997, "Psychosocial Aspects of Breast Cancer Treatment," *Seminars in Oncology*, 24(1), pp. 36–47.

Spiegel, D., J. R. Bloom, and I. Yalom, 1981, "Group Support for Patients with Metastatic Cancer. A Randomized Outcome Study," *Archives of General Psychiatry*, 38(5), pp. 527–33.

Spiegel, D., and R. Moore, 1997, "Imagery and Hypnosis in the Treatment of Cancer Patients," *Oncology (Williston Park, N.Y.)*, 11(8), pp. 1179–89. discussion 1189–1195.

Steel, J. L., D. A. Geller, T. C. Gamblin, M. C. Olek, and B. I. Carr, 2007, "Depression, Immunity, and Survival in Patients with Hepatobiliary Carcinoma," *Journal of Clinical Oncology*, 25(17), pp. 2397–405.

Strommel, M., B. A. Given, and C. W. Given, 2002, "Depression and Functional Status as Predictors of Death Among Cancer Patients," *Cancer* 94, pp. 2719–27.

Syrjala, K. L., and M. E. Chapko, 1995, "Evidence for a Biopsychosocial Model of Cancer Treatment-Related Pain," *Pain*, 61(1), pp. 69–79.

Thaker, P. H., L. Y. Han, A. A. Kamat, J. M. Arevalo, R. Takahashi, C. Lu *et al.*, 2006, "Chronic Stress Promotes Tumor Growth and Angiogenesis in a Mouse Model of Ovarian Carcinoma," *Nature Medicine*, 12(8), pp. 939–44.

Troesch, L. M., C. B. Rodehaver, E. A. Delaney, and B. Yanes, 1993, "The Influence of Guided Imagery on Chemotherapy-Related Nausea and Vomiting," *Oncology Nursing Forum*, 20(8), pp. 1179–85.

Turner-Cobb, J. M., S. E. Sephton, C. Koopman, J. Blake-Mortimer, and D. Spiegel, 2000, "Social Support and Salivary Cortisol in Women with Metastatic Breast Cancer," *Psychosomatic Medicine*, 62(3), pp. 337–45.

Van der Pompe, G., M. H. Antoni, C. L. Mulder, C. Heijnen, K. Goodkin, A. De Graeff *et al.*, 1994, "Psychoneuroimmunology and the Course of Breast Cancer: An Overview. The Impact of Psychosocial Factors on Progression of Breast Cancer Through Immune and Endocrine Mechanisms," *Psychooncology*, 3, pp. 271–88.

Walker, L., M. Walker, and K. Odston, 1999, "Psychological, Clinical and Pathological Effects of Relaxation Training and Guided Imagery During Chemotherapy," *British Journal of Cancer* 80(1–2), pp. 262–8.

Wallace, K. G., 1997, "Analysis of Recent Literature Concerning Relaxation and Imagery Interventions for Cancer Pain," *Cancer Nursing*, 20(2), pp. 79–87.

Wallace, R. K., H. Benson, and A. F. Wilson, 1971, "A Wakeful Hypometabolic Physiologic State," *American Journal of Physiology*, 221(3), pp. 795–9.

Watson, M., J. S. Haviland, S. Greer, J. Davidson, and J. M. Bliss, 1999, "Influence of Psychological Response on Survival in Breast Cancer: A Population-Based Cohort Study," *The Lancet*, 354(9187), pp. 1331–6.

White, David Gordon, 1996, *The Alchemical Body: Sid Traditions in Medieval India*, Chicago and London: Chicago University Press

Zeltzer, L. K., M. J. Dolgin, S. LeBaron, and C. LeBaron, 1991, "A Randomized, Controlled Study of Behavioral Intervention for Chemotherapy Distress in Children with Cancer," *Pediatrics* 88(1), pp. 34–42.

Notes

1. The four main categories that the National Center for Complementary and Alternative Medicine use to define CAM: Mind-body medicine, Biologically based practices, Manipulative and body-based practices, and Energy medicine (http://nccam.nih.gov/health/whatiscam/overview.htm).

2. We also find the use of the term Tibetan Yoga in Evans-Wentz 1935 (rp. 1958), Michael Roach 2004, and Namkhai Norbu 2008, among others.

MEDITATION AS MEDICINE
A Critique

Wakoh Shannon Hickey

Twenty-seven adults are arrayed at the front of a large, sloping lecture hall: some lying on their backs, some upright in free-standing chairs, some in the tiers of seats bolted to the floor. Most appear to range in age from mid-forties to mid-fifties. The lights are dim, most eyes are closed, and except for occasional fidgeting, everyone is silent and still. The instructor, a kindly psychiatrist who bears a striking resemblance to Santa Claus, has instructed everyone to focus attention on the ebb and flow of the breath, counting exhalations from one to eight, then returning to one. Each time the mind wanders off, the meditator should begin counting again at one: the point is not to get to eight, but to continually refocus attention on the breath.

Toward the end of the evening, participants gather on chairs in a circle, each speaking in turn about her or his experience. One woman says she hates meditating, because her mind wanders constantly, and her thoughts are full of "mean" commentary about herself. A Vietnam veteran remarks that for thirty years he feared that "if I allowed myself to have the memories they'd kill me, so I fought them off like I fought the war." Meditation has helped him to see that his thoughts will not kill him, and that facing the painful memories relieves the depression and anxiety caused by his avoidance. Another woman's voice breaks as she remarks that part of her resistance to meditation emerges from a belief that "I don't deserve happiness."

Scenes like this are being repeated in hundreds, perhaps thousands, of settings around the United States. They are part of a program called

Mindfulness-Based Stress Reduction (MBSR), which molecular biologist Jon Kabat-Zinn, Ph.D., developed at the University of Massachusetts Medical Center in 1971. During the eight-week MBSR program, participants attend a two-and-a-half hour class each week. They learn various forms of sitting and walking meditation, do visualizations to cultivate loving-kindness, and practice simple yoga postures. They also agree to complete daily homework assignments: to meditate and do yoga for forty-five minutes each day, and to keep a journal recording these practices and the practitioners' responses to stressful situations.

Other therapeutic protocols employing mindfulness practice have been developed specifically for dealing with psychological problems. Mindfulness-Based Cognitive Therapy (MBCT) has adapted the MBSR program for people suffering from depression.[1] Dialectical Behavioral Therapy (DBT) is a protocol for treating Borderline Personality Disorder developed by psychotherapist Marsha Linehan, Ph.D. It includes a form of mindfulness derived from Zen meditation and seems to be effective for addressing a disorder that is notoriously difficult to treat.[2] For simplicity's sake, this article will focus on MBSR, the largest of the programs.

Meditation as medicine: the scope

The precise scope of MBSR is unknown, because the program is not centrally controlled. In 1996, fifteen years after MBSR was launched in Massachusetts, approximately 120 programs were operating in the U.S., and "a few" in other countries. A year later, the number had more than doubled.[3] As of April 2010, a database hosted by the Center for Mindfulness in Medicine, Healthcare, and Society, which Kabat-Zinn founded, listed 553 MBSR programs around the world. The Center estimates that "tens of thousands" of people worldwide have completed the program.[4] A slew of medical studies on MBSR have linked it to faster recovery from psoriasis outbreaks, improved cardiac health, fewer post-chemotherapy symptoms among cancer patients, greater immune responses to flu vaccine, and increased activity—possibly even neural growth—in areas of the brain associated with positive mood.[5]

I have no doubt that mindfulness can be very helpful to people in a variety of ways. I have practiced it myself for more than twenty-five years and have taught it to others, and I have both experienced and observed its beneficial effects. Yet I have a number of concerns about the way mindfulness practice has become commodified in recent years. I find some of the recent clinical research on meditation very intriguing. Yet I have some questions about the research methods and about how to interpret the resulting data. I will explain those concerns below, but first I want to do two things: to show the dramatic increase in medical research on meditation over the past decade, and to consider some of the rhetorical strategies that underlie this increase. Then, I will offer five critiques of MBSR and the booming industry in meditation-as-medicine.

Over the past thirty years, literally thousands of books and articles describing psychological and physiological effects of meditation have been published.[6] Since 1972, the federal government has funded hundreds of research studies dealing with various forms of meditation. In fiscal years 2008 and 2009 alone, it spent nearly $51 million on this research. Initially, scientists studied the effects of Transcendental Meditation, as taught by the Indian guru Maharishi Mahesh Yogi. Today, most studies employ some form of mindfulness meditation—most often MBSR, MBCT, or DBT. A handful of studies employ other forms of meditation, and some do not specify the type of meditation or mindfulness practice.[7] This is one of the problems with the research: "meditation" is not well defined.

In the chart at Figure 1, the solid line represents medical research on all types of meditation funded by the United States government since 1998. It funded seven studies that year, eighty-nine in 2008, and 122 in

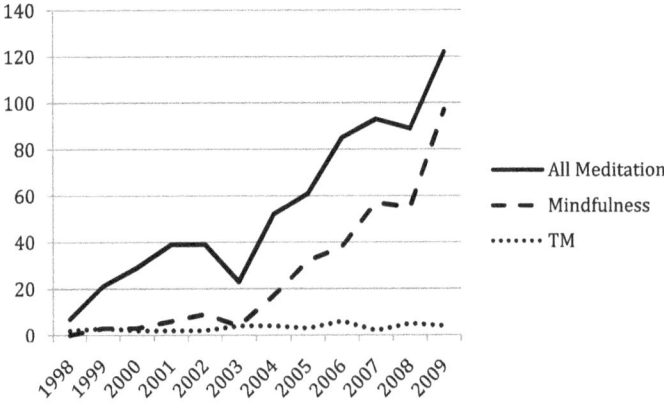

Figure 1. Federally funded research on meditation 1998–2009.

2009.[8] The dashed line represents research studies that specifically identify mindfulness, and the dotted line represents those that explicitly identify Transcendental Meditation. In 2009, the government funded four studies of TM and ninety-seven studies of mindfulness (all types).

These are just federally funded research studies. Next, let us look more broadly at clinical trials: funded publicly, or privately, or both. As of late January 2010, the National Institutes of Health was tracking 132 clinical trials dealing with meditation of all types, of which sixty-one were recruiting or preparing to recruit volunteers, thirty were actively underway, and forty were complete. (One had withdrawn.) Among those, 113 trials studied some form of mindfulness and fifty-seven dealt with MBSR. Thirty-two trials employed MBCT, and fifteen employed DBT.[9] Thus, 79 percent of studies dealing with meditation and 92 percent of those dealing with mindfulness used one of these three protocols.

"Buddhist meditation (without the Buddhism)"
Jon Kabat-Zinn has said explicitly that he wants to promote meditation in a way that does not scare people off by associating it with unfamiliar religious practices and Buddhist technical terminology. When he began to develop MBSR in 1971, he anticipated that doctors and scientists, as well as many patients, would resist a program explicitly grounded in a particular religious tradition, especially a foreign one. Indeed, over the past century or more, orthodox physicians have regularly denounced promoters of alternative medicine as quacks or charlatans. So it is understandable that Kabat-Zinn's rhetoric has carefully distanced MBSR from Buddhist and Hindu teachings that regard meditation and yoga as religious disciplines. He calls the mindfulness practice taught in MBSR "Buddhist meditation (without the Buddhism)."[10]

Expressing another pragmatic concern, Kabat-Zinn has said: "[I]f you want to be able to integrate into medicine … you've got to be able to charge the insurance companies for this."[11] To reach his intended audiences effectively, "[T]he language that we use … is how to take better care of yourself; how to live more skillfully and more fully; how to move toward greater levels of health and well-being." He also stresses that MBSR is "a complement to medical treatment, not a substitute for it."[12]

When asked at a conference on American Buddhism whether MBSR might be misappropriating Buddhist traditions, Kabat-Zinn said, "I really don't care about Buddhism. It's an interesting religion but it's not what I most care about. What I value in Buddhism is that it brought me to the Dharma."[13] Although he has been involved in explicitly Buddhist meditation practices for several decades, he can make this rather striking remark because he has defined the key term, "Dharma," as trans-religious, trans-cultural, and trans-historic.

He says, "The word *Dharma*, to me, is pointing to something that really is universal.... The cultural and ideological overlays, and the historical elements of [Buddhism], beautiful and honorable and wonderful as they are, are not necessarily the heart of the Dharma, which transcends them."[14]

Two problematic assumptions

Kabat-Zinn's remark is based on two assumptions that I want to challenge. The first is the assumption that the central practice of Buddhism is, and has always been, meditation. Although this is a common perception among Americans, any careful study of Buddhist history will reveal that meditation has almost always been a specialty of a small minority of monks and nuns.[15] Most Buddhist practices have centered on devotion and generating merit (or good karma) for oneself and one's ancestors. The focus on meditation, especially among laypeople, is at most a century and a half old, in a tradition that spans more than two and a half millennia. It has become widespread only in the past fifty years or so. The second faulty assumption is that Buddhist or Hindu religious ideas or practices are universal, transcending any particular cultural or historical context. Scholars of religion, including scholars of Buddhism, have pointed out that this perennialism itself is a product of modern, Euro-American colonialism.[16]

Kabat-Zinn's assumptions about meditation and the universality of Dharma place him squarely in a cultural, historical, and religious context that includes Swedenborgianism, Mesmerism, Transcendentalism, pragmatism, Theosophy, and New Thought. These Western metaphysical traditions interacted with modernist re-interpretations of Buddhism and Hinduism in Asia, which were produced in response to particular historical, political, religious, and economic conditions in Asia. As a result of these interactions, we tend nowadays to talk about how meditation and yoga can improve physical and mental health, rather about how they can help us to deconstruct the "self," realize Nirvana, and/or prevent negative future rebirths. But Kabat-Zinn, like other contemporary promoters of meditation-as-medicine, is silent about (or perhaps unaware of) this history.[17] Robert Sharf, a respected scholar of Buddhism, commented,

> [I]t will take a long time—perhaps centuries—for the West to engage with the Buddhist tradition at a deeper level. Such an engagement will require that we see past the confines of our own historical and cultural situation and gain a greater appreciation of the depth and complexity of the Buddhist heritage. Certainly one impediment to that is the idea that the only thing that matters is meditation and that everything else is just excess baggage.[18]

So my first objection to Kabat-Zinn's rhetoric is that it is, at best, myopic. At worst, it may be intellectually dishonest. I understand why he uses the rhetorical strategies he does, and I can see how they might seem necessary to accomplish the larger goal of making a helpful practice more accessible to people who might never try it otherwise—a goal that I applaud. But this rhetoric also erases two or three millennia of Hindu and Buddhist history—and the monks, nuns, monarchs, nobles, and ordinary laypeople who preserved and developed it. Kabat-Zinn himself learned mindfulness from Buddhist teachers, in Buddhist communities. I do not actually think there is anything inherently wrong with practicing meditation or yoga or lovingkindness for better wellbeing. It is recognized as a legitimate goal within these traditions, albeit a lesser one than enlightenment or union with Brahman. What I am critiquing here is a rhetorical erasure of the past, and the assumption that one's own social, cultural, and historical perspective applies universally.

My second concern is that MBSR separates meditation and yoga not just from their doctrinal contexts, but from their moral frameworks. In both religious traditions, moral conduct is the foundation of meditation practice, because one cannot have peace of mind if one's behavior is unethical. In Buddhism, lay practitioners are expected to observe five basic moral precepts: not killing, lying, stealing, engaging in sexual misconduct, or intoxicating oneself or others. Buddhist monks and nuns adopt additional precepts, numbering from ten to more than 300, depending upon the tradition and, in some cases, the gender of the practitioner. (In some orders, nuns take more vows than monks.) Exemplary conduct is what makes monks and nuns worthy of the honorific title "Venerable," and that is why it is considered meritorious for laypeople to make donations to the monastic Sangha. Doing so generates positive karma. The purpose of moral conduct is to overcome greed, hatred, and ignorance, and move along the Path toward enlightenment. Moral conduct (*yama* and *niyama*) is also the foundational practice of yoga, according to the Eight Limbs of Yoga developed by Patanjali. The ultimate purpose of yoga is to realize union with the Divine. In MBSR, participants in the day-long meditation retreats that are part of the training may be asked to observe the five Buddhist precepts for laypeople on that particular day. But moral conduct is not typically part of MBSR training; these stipulations are not universal; and they were not part of the courses I will discuss in the following paragraphs. Furthermore, although the Center for Mindfulness offers training and certification programs for MBSR teachers, and recommends both ongoing meditation practice and graduate-level education in a relevant discipline, it does not regulate teachers or require any certification to teach the program.[19]

Nor is community central to MBSR training, which is my third concern. The program, like the American Vipassana movement that underlies it, is highly individualistic. In Buddhist practice, as in many other religious disciplines, community is central. Even hermits depend upon a community for food. Community, or sangha, is one of the Three Treasures of Buddhism. MBSR, on the other hand, consists of classes, workshops, retreats, books, and audio materials that individuals buy. In class sessions, students spend very little time interacting with one another, so relationships have little opportunity to form. Students' formal relationship with the teacher ends when the course ends. One consequence of this individualistic structure is that people may stop practicing once the course ends, which obviously limits its effectiveness.

In two MBSR classes that were part of a research study at Duke University, participants reported a significant drop in the amount of meditation they did after they completed the course. Many stopped meditating altogether without the support of weekly class meetings. Of the fifty-six people who originally enrolled in the study, only twenty-four completed the program and showed up for the follow-up assessment eight weeks later. On average, they reported meditating about half as much as they had during the class. Meditation is very difficult to maintain on one's own, especially when difficult emotions or memories arise.

A fourth problem is that MBSR stresses individual practice as the key to wellbeing, so it tends to avoid any analysis of the systemic or institutional causes of suffering. These include racism, sexism, and poverty, all of which can affect access to medical care, at least in the United States. Kabat-Zinn is clearly aware of and concerned about these issues,[20] but the program itself is individualistic. This inattention to systemic suffering is a feature MBSR shares with metaphysical religions that promote positive thinking or the so-called "prosperity gospel." If you are suffering, it is your individual psychological problem.

One reason for this in MBSR may be the socio-economic status of people who take the courses. In most cases, the program is only fully accessible to people who can spare several hundred dollars and devote about eight hours a week to it for two months. In the Duke study just mentioned, MBSR classes were offered free of charge, in part to attract people who otherwise could not afford the normal fee of $370 to $395.[21] Nevertheless, 35 percent of the participants recruited reported annual incomes over $65,000. Only 4 percent had incomes below $20,000. And yet, according to the most recent available data from Durham County, approximately 22 percent of local adults had incomes below the federal poverty level of $9,750. Among women, 32.5 percent of those without children and 38 percent of those with children had incomes below the poverty line.[22]

Of those who took a Duke MBSR course in the spring of 2007, 85 percent had college or graduate-level education. Twenty-three percent had college degrees; 11 percent reported some graduate-level education; and 51 percent had graduate degrees. And although the population of Durham County was 48 percent white and 38.5 percent black, 91 percent of the MBSR participants were white. While these results cannot be generalized to all participants of MBSR courses, they do suggest sharp disparities between the general population of Durham and the people taking MBSR courses there.[23]

If this demographic profile does hold true more generally, however, then perhaps one reason the program does not include systemic analyses of illness and other forms of suffering is that the people involved are less afflicted by racism and poverty, which are systemic problems affecting health and access to medical care.[24]

My fifth and final critique has to do with methodological problems associated with medical research on meditation. Some of the studies are quite intriguing. Yet peer-reviewed journals have noted a variety of methodological concerns. These include inadequate controls, small sample sizes, demographic homogeneity among participants, and inattention to gender as a variable. In response to such critiques, researchers have attempted to improve their study designs. Some more recent review articles have reiterated the need for methodological rigor but are more positive about the results.[25] Although meditation may not be sufficient or appropriate for some people (e.g., those suffering from severe post-traumatic stress, major depression, or psychosis), mindfulness, *in conjunction with medication*, does seem to be helpful to those who have difficulty regulating their emotions.

Brain research on meditators is more problematic. Again, some findings are very intriguing. Certainly, the images produced by PET scans and functional MRIs of meditators appear to be very clear and compelling. Yet we must bear in mind that at every stage of production, these images are generated in a "black box" of assumptions, technical procedures, and human factors that we cannot see.[26] For example, extraordinary results depend upon comparison to a theoretical "normal" result, but "normal" is very difficult to define. In studies of brain activity using PET scans (positron-emission tomography, which creates three-dimensional images of the brain by tracing movements of radioactive isotopes), "normal" typically means a right-handed white male. This means that variations in race, gender, left-handedness (and possibly age) could produce different results. In addition, scans of research subjects' brains are compared to a hypothetical "average" brain—a mathematical model that can vary from laboratory to laboratory. Brain activity also varies according to factors such as time of day, and whether the subject has recently ingested substances such as caffeine or nicotine. Because the imaging technology is expensive, sample sizes are typically small, which affects the degree to which particular results can be generalized.

Data from scans are translated into colored images, an interpretive process that is not necessarily consistent from study to study, and that inevitably highlights some differences and downplays others. A focus on activity in a particular area of the brain also tends to obscure the ways that brain functions may be distributed across several areas simultaneously. The "resting" state between activities under study may be defined inconsistently from study to study as well, which affects how results are compared. (And, as has been noted, "meditation" is not defined consistently or well in clinical research.) The interpretation of images requires cooperation across multiple scientific disciplines, among researchers who have different types and degrees of expertise, and possibly competing agendas when it comes to issues like publication credit, research funding, and career advancement. Although the images may be very effective rhetorically, the more carefully one peers into the black box, the more problematic the images become. It is important to be honest about these limitations—even if it makes research funding a bit more difficult to obtain.

At the 2005 Mind and Life Institute conference on the clinical applications of meditation, the Dalai Lama was regaled with information about the latest clinical research on mindfulness. After the final presentation, he remarked: "For me, analytical meditation is more useful." He explained, through his translator, that it is important to analyze the source of one's pain. Often it is rooted in an effort to grasp at impermanence, or in self-centeredness, or in an unrealistic view of one's situation. Each of these problems requires a different kind of approach, he said, without elaborating. His final remark produced peals of laughter but was also telling: "In order to use your intelligence more effectively, I prefer sound sleep better than meditation."[27]

Advocates of mindfulness training argue that its transformative power lies in its ability to help people notice their subconscious internal narratives more clearly, and free themselves from destructive habits of mind. It helps them to be more fully present and more compassionate with themselves and with others, which promotes healing. I agree completely. Again, I practice mindfulness and I teach it to others—usually in a non-religious way, and always free of charge.[28] I also agree that it is appropriate to "meet people where they are" when offering a practice that can foster liberation from mental habits that create suffering. Buddhist tradition acknowledges that people have different motives for practice and are at different stages of development. I have no objection to meditation teachers doing outreach into new settings, and offering a beneficial practice to people who might otherwise never set foot in a meditation hall. I think mindfulness can be helpful to people of any religion, and to those who are non-religious.

What I find objectionable is the tendency to turn this discipline into a *commodity* for sale. To do so risks fostering the very attitudes—greed and individualism—that both Buddhist and yogic traditions assert are inimical to liberation.

I also believe long-term formation in religious community can be very valuable, to the extent that it encourages us to grapple with problems we might otherwise avoid facing, such as our own self-centeredness or unwillingness to forgive, and the challenges of welcoming and working with people we might not like or understand. (Granted, not all religious communities do this.) Communities can also offer support and help us to find meaning during periods of difficulty—which, as some clinical research suggests, can be good for people's overall health and happiness.

While I applaud the desire to foster healing that drives many promoters of meditation-as-medicine, I also have the concerns I have enumerated here: myopic rhetoric, the removal of meditation practice from its moral and communal frameworks, a tendency toward individualism and commodification, and questions about research methodologies. Above all, while a therapeutic approach to meditation is well suited to modern consumer capitalism, it does not necessarily contribute to addressing broader social problems that affect psychological and physical health, or access to medical care. For that we need to think systemically about the dynamics of race, gender, and class—and their effects in our political system, as recent debates over medical insurance reform amply demonstrate. We must grapple with those issues collectively, and work collectively for systemic change. In doing so, we need historical and cultural perspective. In short: we need people who are embedded in their communities and actively engaged in trying to make them healthier.

Works cited

Allen, Nicholas B., Richard Chambers, Wendy Knight, and Melbourne Academic Mindfulness Interest Group, 2006, "Mindfulness-Based Psychotherapies: A Review of Conceptual Foundations, Empirical Evidence and Practical Considerations." *Australian & New Zealand Journal of Psychiatry* 40(4), pp. 285–94.

Baer, Ruth A., 2003, "Mindfulness Training as a Clinical Intervention: A Conceptual and Empirical Review." *Clinical Psychology: Science and Practice* 10(2), pp. 125–43.

Bishop, S. R., 2002, "What Do We Really Know About Mindfulness-Based Stress Reduction?" *Psychosomatic Medicine* 64, pp. 71–83.

Brown, Kirk Warren, and Richard M. Ryan, 2003, "The Benefits of Being Present: Mindfulness and Its Role in Psychological Well-Being." *Journal of Personality & Social Psychology* 84(4), pp. 822–48.

Davidson, R. J., J. Kabat-Zinn, J. Schumacher, M. Rosenkranz, D. Muller, S. Santorelli, F. Urbanowski, A. Harrington, K. Bonus, and J. Sheridan, 2003, "Alterations in Brain and Immune Function Produced by Mindfulness Meditation." *Psychosomatic Medicine* 65, pp. 564–70.

Dumit, Joseph, 2004, "Producing Brain Images of Mind," in *Picturing Personhood: Brain Scans and Biomedical Identity*, Princeton, NJ: Princeton University Press, pp. 53–105.

Hickey, Wakoh Shannon, 2008, "Mind Cure, Meditation, and Medicine: Hidden Histories of Mental Healing in the United States." Ph.D. diss., Duke University.

Hoppes, Kimberly, 2006, "The Application of Mindfulness-Based Cognitive Interventions in the Treatment of Co-Occurring Addictive and Mood Disorders." *CNS Spectrums* 11(11), pp. 829–51.

Jarrell, Howard R., 1985, *International Meditation Bibliography 1950–1982*. Vol. 12, ATLA Bibliography Series, Metuchen, NJ and London: The American Theological Library Association and The Scarecrow Press, Inc.

Kabat-Zinn, Jon, 1994. *Wherever You Go There You Are*. New York: Hyperion

Kabat-Zinn, Jon, 1998, "Toward the Mainstreaming of American Dharma Practice," in Al Rapaport, and Brian D. Hotchkiss ed., *Buddhism in America: The Official Record of the Landmark Conference on the Future of Buddhist Meditative Practices in the West*, Boston, January 17-19, 1997, Rutland, VT: Charles E. Tuttle, Co., pp. 478–528.

Kabat-Zinn, Jon, 2000, "Indra's Net at Work: The Mainstreaming of Dharma Practice in Society," in Gay Watson and Stephen Batchelor, eds., *The Psychology of Awakening: Buddhism, Science, and Our Day to Day Lives*, York Beach, ME: S. Weiser, pp. 225–49.

Kabat-Zinn, Jon, 2005, *Coming to Our Senses: Healing Ourselves and the World through Mindfulness*. 1st ed. New York: Hyperion.

Kabat-Zinn, Jon, and University of Massachusetts Medical Center/Worcester, Stress Reduction Clinic, 1991. *Full Catastrophe Living: Using the Wisdom of Your Body and Mind to Face Stress, Pain, and Illness*. New York: Delta.

Leuchter, A. F. et al., 2002, "Changes in Brain Function of Depressed Subjects During Treatment with Placebo." *American Journal of Psychiatry* 160(2), pp. 387–8.

Linehan, Marsha, 1993, *Cognitive-Behavioral Treatment of Borderline Personality Disorder*. New York: Guilford Press.

Lopez, Donald S., Jr., 2008, *Buddhism & Science: A Guide for the Perplexed*. Chicago: University of Chicago Press.

Lutz, A., L. L Greischar, N. B. Rawlings, M. Ricard, and R. J. Davidson, 2004, "Long-Term Meditators Self-Induce High-Amplitude Gamma Synchrony During Mental Practice." *Proceedings of the National Academy of Sciences* 101, pp. 16369–73.

McMahan, David L., 2008, *The Making of Buddhist Modernism*. New York: Oxford University Press.

Monro, Robin, A. K. Ghosh, and Daniel Kalish, 1989. *Yoga Research Bibliography: Scientific Studies on Yoga and Meditation*. Cambridge, UK: Yoga Biomedical Trust.

Murphy, Michael, and Steven Donovan, 1999, *The Physical and Psychological Effects of Meditation: A Review of Contemporary Research with a Comprehensive Bibliography 1931-1996*, in Eugene Taylor, ed. 2nd ed. Sausalito, CA: Institute of Noetic Sciences.

Ott, Mary Jane, Rebecca L. Norris, and Susan M. Bauer-Wu, 2006, "Mindfulness Meditation for Oncology Patients: A Discussion and Critical Review." *Integrative Cancer Therapies* 5(2), pp. 98–108.

Payne, Richard K., 2007, "Traditionalist Representations of Buddhism," in *American Academy of Religion Annual Meeting, Buddhism in the West Consultation*. San Diego, CA, forthcoming in *Pacific World*.

Roepstorff, Andreas, 2004, "Mapping Brain Mappers, an Ethnographic Coda" in R. Frackowiak et al. eds., *Human Brain Function*. London: Elsevier, pp. 1105–17.

Schmidt, Stefan, 2004, "Mindfulness and Healing Intention: Concepts, Practice, and Research Evaluation." *Journal of Alternative & Complementary Medicine* 10(Suppl. 1), pp. S7–14.

Sharf, Robert H., 1995a, "Buddhist Modernism and the Rhetoric of Meditative Experience." *Numen* 42, pp. 228–83.

Sharf, Robert H., 1995b, "Sanbōkyōdan: Zen and the Way of the New Religions." *Japanese Journal of Religious Studies* 22(3–4), pp. 417–57.

Sharf, Robert H., and Andrew Cooper, 2007, "Losing Our Religion." *Tricycle: The Buddhist Review* 64(Summer 2007), pp. 44–9.

Notes

1. See http://www.mbct.com, accessed January 29, 2010.
2. Marsha Linehan, *Cognitive-Behavioral Treatment of Borderline Personality Disorder*, Diagnosis and Treatment of Mental Disorders (New York: Guilford Press, 1993). See also http://behavioraltech.org. Linehan is a student of Willigis Jäger, OSB, a Benedictine monk who

also received authorization as a Zen teacher in the Sanbō-Kyōdan school of Zen, a modern movement that has been active in Buddhist-Christian dialogue. Although marginal in Japan, Sanbō-Kyōdan has been extremely influential in American Zen. Jäger left Sanbō-Kyōdan in 2009 to found his own organization. http://www.willigis-jaeger.de/en/?Zen: New_Line_of_Zen and http://www.ciolek.com/WWWVLPages/ZenPages/HaradaYasutani.html, both accessed January 29, 2010. See also Robert H. Sharf, "Sanbōkyōdan: Zen and the Way of the New Religions," *Japanese Journal of Religious Studies* 22, no. 3–4 (1995).

3. Jon Kabat-Zinn, "Indra's Net at Work: The Mainstreaming of Dharma Practice in Society," in *The Psychology of Awakening: Buddhism, Science, and Our Day to Day Lives*, ed. Gay Watson and Stephen Batchelor (York Beach, ME: S. Weiser, 2000), 239–40.

4. The directory of programs may be found at http://www.umassmed.edu/cfm/mbsr/index.cfm, accessed April 9, 2010.

5. Links to much of this research can be found at http://psyphz.psych.wisc.edu/web/pubs/pubs_articles.html#2009. Some representative examples include: S. R. Bishop, "What Do We Really Know About Mindfulness-Based Stress Reduction?" *Psychosomatic Medicine* 64(2002); R. J. Davidson and J. Kabat-Zinn et al., "Alterations in Brain and Immune Function Produced by Mindfulness Meditation," *Psychosomatic Medicine*, no. 65 (2003); A. F. Leuchter et al., "Changes in Brain Function of Depressed Subjects During Treatment with Placebo," *American Journal of Psychiatry* 160, no. 2 (2002); A. Lutz et al., "Long-Term Meditators Self-Induce High-Amplitude Gamma Synchrony During Mental Practice," *Proceedings of the National Academy of Sciences* 101 (2004); Michael Murphy and Steven Donovan, *The Physical and Psychological Effects of Meditation: A Review of Contemporary Research with a Comprehensive Bibliography 1931–1996*, ed. Eugene Taylor, 2nd ed. (Sausalito, CA: Institute of Noetic Sciences, 1999). See also Jon Kabat-Zinn, *Wherever You Go There You Are* (New York: Hyperion, 1994); Michael Murphy and Steven Donovan, "Toward the Mainstreaming of American Dharma Practice," in *Buddhism in America: The Official Record of the Landmark Conference on the Future of Buddhist Meditative Practices in the West, Boston, January 17–19, 1997*, ed. Al Rapaport and Brian D. Hotchkiss (Rutland, VT: Charles E. Tuttle, Co., 1998); Michael Murphy and Steven Donovan, *Coming to Our Senses: Healing Ourselves and the World through Mindfulness*, 1st ed. (New York: Hyperion, 2005); Jon Kabat-Zinn and University of Massachusetts Medical Center/Worcester Stress Reduction Clinic, *Full Catastrophe Living: Using the Wisdom of Your Body and Mind to Face Stress, Pain, and Illness* (New York: Delta, 1991).

6. Murphy and Donovan, *The Physical and Psychological Effects of Meditation: A Review of Contemporary Research with a Comprehensive Bibliography 1931–1996*, 153–277. Most of the references are articles in peer-reviewed academic and scientific journals; a few are books oriented toward more general audiences. Of the studies published before 1970, most were authored in the 1960s by Indian researchers studying physiological effects of yoga and by Japanese researchers studying effects of Zen meditation. A bibliography published more than a decade earlier by the American Theological Library Association included more than 2,200 entries, including 937 articles in journals and magazines; more than 1,000 books in English, German, French, Spanish, and Portuguese; 200 dissertations and theses; 32 motion pictures; 93 sound recordings; and 32 societies and associations, Howard R. Jarrell, *International Meditation Bibliography 1950–1982*, vol. 12, ATLA Bibliography Series (Metuchen, NJ and London: The American Theological Library Association and The Scarecrow Press, Inc.,

1985). A 1989 bibliography on studies of yoga and meditation lists 1275 articles; 31 books, dissertations, and reports; and 292 conferences, symposia, and seminars. Robin Monro, A.K. Ghosh, and Daniel Kalish, *Yoga Research Bibliography: Scientific Studies on Yoga and Meditation* (Cambridge, UK: Yoga Biomedical Trust, 1989).

7. The National Institutes of Health maintains a database of federally funded research from 1985 to the present, called Research Portfolio Online Reporting Tool (RePORT). It is available at http://projectreporter.nih.gov/reporter.cfm. This database replaced the CRISP database (Computer Retrieval of Information on Scientific Projects) on September 1, 2009. CRISP was available at http://crisp.cit.nih.gov/ until October 31, 2009, at which time it was discontinued. CRISP data went back to 1972. Both databases include(d) projects funded by multiple agencies. Searches of both RePORT and CRISP on October 18 and 23, 2009, for studies with the keywords "meditation" or "mindfulness," revealed a total of 434 projects from 1972 to date, many of which were or are multi-year projects. The RePORT database is updated weekly, and now includes additional data. Searches on January 29, 2010, of the period from 1985 to date revealed 685 studies involving either meditation or mindfulness. The multi-year projects were each counted as individual projects for purposes of these tallies.

8. http://projectreporter.nih.gov/reporter.cfm. Accessed January 29, 2010.

9. http://clinicaltrials.gov/ct2/search, accessed January 29, 2010. Among the MBSR studies, 33 were recruiting, 16 were actively underway, and 13 were complete. Among the MBCT studies, 21 were recruiting, 7 were active, and 4 were complete. Among the DBT studies, 8 were recruiting, 4 were active, 2 were complete, and one had suspended operations.

10. Kabat-Zinn, "Toward the Mainstreaming of American Dharma Practice," 481.

11. Ibid., 505.

12. Ibid., 487.

13. Ibid., 515.

14. Ibid., 495.

15. A number of respected scholars of Buddhism have pointed this out. One recent example is Donald S. Lopez Jr., *Buddhism & Science: A Guide for the Perplexed* (Chicago: University of Chicago Press, 2008), 207–10. See also the references in note 16, below.

16. Richard K. Payne, "Traditionalist Representations of Buddhism," presented at American Academy of Religion Annual Meeting, Buddhism in the West Consultation (San Diego, CA 2007, forthcoming in *Pacific World*), 5–6. See also Robert H. Sharf, "Buddhist Modernism and the Rhetoric of Meditative Experience," *Numen* 42 (1995). For an excellent, extended discussion of "Meditation and Modernity," and of modern deployments of mindfulness meditation, see David L. McMahan, *The Making of Buddhist Modernism* (New York: Oxford University Press, 2008), 183–240.

17. Wakoh Shannon Hickey, "Mind Cure, Meditation, and Medicine: Hidden Histories of Mental Healing in the United States" (Ph.D. diss., Duke University, 2008).

18. Robert H. Sharf and Andrew Cooper, "Losing Our Religion," *Tricycle: The Buddhist Review* 64, (Summer 2007).

19. http://www.umassmed.edu/cfm/oasis/index.aspx, accessed January 30, 2010.

20. Kabat-Zinn, *Coming to Our Senses: Healing Ourselves and the World through Mindfulness*.

21. In its regular, fee-based MBSR courses, the Duke Center for Integrative Medicine offers some scholarships, but does not accept medical insurance to cover course tuition.

22. The remaining 58 percent of MBSR participants fell within the broad range of incomes between $20,000 and $65,000. E-mail from Duke MBSR researcher Andrew Ekblad to Shannon Hickey March 3, 2008. Telephone conversation between Andrew Ekblad and Shannon Hickey March 5, 2008. These data were collected in late 2006 and early 2007, but not analyzed until 2008. Durham poverty figures from 2005 can be found at http://www.durhamnc.gov/departments/eed/income_char.cfm. Accessed October 25, 2009. Federal poverty guidelines for 2005 can be found at http://aspe.hhs.gov/poverty/05poverty.shtml. Accessed October 25, 2009. According to 2007 estimates by http://www.city-data.com, poverty rates in the City of Durham were 18.3 percent for all white residents, and 21.4 percent for all black residents. http://www.city-data.com/city/Durham-North-Carolina.html. Accessed October 25, 2009. For racial data, see http://www.city-data.com/county/Durham_County-NC.html. Accessed October 25, 2009. For 2000 census data on Durham, see http://www.durhamnc.gov/departments/planning/pdf/demographics.pdf. Accessed March 5, 2008.

23. 2007 MBSR Outcomes Study, Duke Center for Integrative Medicine, Principal Investigator Clive Robins, Ph.D. Results are as yet unpublished. These figures were provided in an electronic mail message from researcher Andrew Ekblad to Shannon Hickey, March 3, 2008; and in a telephone conversation between Ekblad and Hickey on March 5, 2008.

24. Another disparity within the world of meditation as meditation is the gender of its most visible spokespersons versus that of MBSR teachers and students. Most of the visible promoters in this field are white men with formal academic credentials, typically from elite institutions. This is not surprising, but it does obscure the role of women in spreading and popularizing the actual practice. At a 2005 conference on "The Science and Clinical Applications of Meditation," sponsored by the Mind and Life Institute in Washington, D.C., all but one of the fourteen individual presenters was male. http://www.investigatingthemind.org/speakers.html Accessed October 28, 2009. At an October 2007 conference at Emory University, called "Mindfulness, Compassion, and the Treatment of Depression," the featured speakers included eleven men and one woman. http://www.mindandlife.org/mlxv.brochure.pdf pp. 9–13. Accessed October 28, 2009. In April 2008, another conference on clinical applications of meditation was held at the Mayo Clinic in Rochester, Minnesota. Other than the Dalai Lama, his translator, and one other Buddhist monk who spoke at Emory, all of the panelists were white. http://www.mindandlife.org/mayo08.brochure.pdf pp. 9–11. Accessed October 28, 2009. But among MBSR teachers in the United States, women outnumber men by more than two to one. (Determined by reviewing the names of teachers listed in the database at http://www.umassmed.edu/cfm/mbsr/, identifying those whose names are typically feminine or masculine, and checking biographical data where available.) See Hickey, "Mind Cure, Meditation, and Medicine," ibid., 182. Although general demographic data about MBSR students is not available, in the Duke courses discussed in this essay, 84 percent of the participants were women. ibid.

25. Bishop, "What Do We Really Know About Mindfulness-Based Stress Reduction?" ibid. Allen, N. B.; R. Chambers; W. Knight, and Melbourne Academic Mindfulness Interest Group, "Mindfulness-Based Psychotherapies: A Review of Conceptual Foundations, Empirical Evidence and Practical Considerations." *Australian & New Zealand Journal of Psychiatry* 40, no. 4 (2006); Ruth A. Baer, "Mindfulness Training as a Clinical Intervention: A Conceptual and

Empirical Review," *Clinical Psychology: Science and Practice* 10, no. 2 (2003); Kirk Warren Brown and Richard M. Ryan, "The Benefits of Being Present: Mindfulness and Its Role in Psychological Well-Being," *Journal of Personality & Social Psychology* 84, no. 4 (2003); Kimberly Hoppes, "The Application of Mindfulness-Based Cognitive Interventions in the Treatment of Co-Occurring Addictive and Mood Disorders," *CNS Spectrums* 11, no. 11 (2006); Mary Jane Ott, Rebecca L. Norris, and Susan M. Bauer-Wu, "Mindfulness Meditation for Oncology Patients: A Discussion and Critical Review," *Integrative Cancer Therapies* 5, no. 2 (2006); Stefan Schmidt, "Mindfulness and Healing Intention: Concepts, Practice, and Research Evaluation," *Journal of Alternative & Complementary Medicine* 10 Suppl. 1(2004).

26. Joseph Dumit, "Producing Brain Images of Mind," in *Picturing Personhood: Brain Scans and Biomedical Identity* (Princeton, NJ: Princeton University Press, 2004). My thanks to Barry Saunders, M.D., Ph.D., of the University of North Carolina-Chapel Hill School of Medicine, for bringing these issues to my attention. Mellon-Sawyer Seminar: Human Being, Human Diversity, and Human Welfare, A Cross-Disciplinary and Cross-Cultural Study in Culture, Science, and Medicine, at the Franklin Humanities Institute, Duke University, March 19, 2007. See also Andreas Roepstorff, "Mapping Brain Mappers, an Ethnographic Coda," in *Human Brain Function*, ed. R. Frackowiak et al. (London: Elsevier, 2004). Thanks to Richard Jaffe, Ph.D., of Duke University, for bringing the latter to my attention.

27. *Highlights from the Science and Clinical Applications of Meditation Conference: An Overview of the Investigating the Mind 2005 Meeting with the Dalai Lama* (Washington, DC: Mind and Life Institute, Mind and Life XIII, 2007), CD-ROM. These remarks occur at the end of the concluding presentation by Ralph Snyderman, M.D., of Duke University Medical Center.

28. Although I am ordained as a Zen priest, full ordination and authorization as a Zen teacher occurs in multiple stages. I am not yet authorized as a Zen teacher. I am authorized as an academic teacher, and regard that as my vocation. In the academic courses I offer, I teach the larger doctrinal and moral frameworks of Buddhist and Hindu meditation in a critical, historical, and comparative manner. Outside of class, I offer meditation instruction in various religious and non-religious settings—without charge. As a priest, I am bound by a set of vows; my practice is supervised by a Zen teacher (Rev. Gengo Akiba, the Sōtō-shū bishop emeritus for North America); and I belong to a Zen community.

THE BUDDHIST HEALTH STUDY
Meditation on Love and Compassion as Features of Religious Practice

Bruce M. Sullivan, Bill Wiist, and Heidi Wayment

> Love and compassion are most important, most precious, most powerful, and most sacred. Practicing them is useful not only in terms of true religion but also in worldly life for both mental and physical health. They are the basic elements supporting our life and happiness. With practice, they become effective and beneficial driving forces for life. (Dalai Lama 2005: 209)

A striking feature of contemporary religion is the growth of Buddhist practices and institutions in the Western world, particularly in Europe and North America. Empirical data, however, are scarce, so considerable disagreement is found regarding the scope of that growth. Some countries include census questions on religious affiliation, and others (such as the United States) do not, so even the most basic data are sporadic and impressionistic.[1] Buddhist organizations do not keep records of membership in a consistent way, nor do they use comparable criteria to determine who is a member. With regard to such limitations, Janet McLellan states, "Although thousands of Buddhist temples, meditation centers, and Buddhist associations can be identified in North America, ... there is no adequate means to determine an accurate count of Buddhists."[2]

In an effort to contribute to the understanding of contemporary Western Buddhism, an interdisciplinary team of researchers at Northern Arizona University wrote a set of questions to elicit data from Buddhist practitioners. In addition to demographic questions, we included

questions on health and health-related practices, and psychological characteristics, drawing from previously used measures (see Wiist et al. 2010). For the Buddhist practices segment of the survey, all the questions were written by the researchers. With the religious practices segment of the survey, we sought (among other things) to test four hypotheses concerning contemporary Western Buddhist practitioners:
1. Contemporary Western Buddhist practitioners are more likely to identify themselves as Buddhist than as members of other religious traditions and to have marked that identity in a formal way such as pronouncing the Three Refuges formula.
2. Contemporary Western Buddhist practitioners are more likely to engage in meditation than to attend Buddhist religious services supervised by clergy.
3. Contemporary Western Buddhist practitioners who engage in meditation are more likely to engage in a variety of meditative practices, practices that they regard as identifiably distinct, than to engage in a single meditative technique.
4. Buddhist practitioners today engage in conscious efforts to increase loving-kindness and compassion through meditation practices.

Method and Data
The questionnaire totaled 265 questions. Once it was written and tested for validity and clarity by three professors of religious studies who have expertise in Buddhism, the questionnaire was placed on a website. We invited members of an assortment of Buddhist organizations to participate in this survey beginning August 2007 and ending January 2008 (six months altogether). In an effort to reach scholars and practitioners of Buddhism, we put the invitation onto three listservs: RISA-L (the Religion in South Asia list), H-Buddhism, and Buddha-L. We e-mailed some 270 Buddhist organizations that have websites and e-mail addresses we could find; some of these are multinational, even global, organizations. We asked these organizations to circulate our invitation to the survey among their members, and some forwarded the e-mail and/or placed the invitation on their own websites. We also paid for some advertisements (with grant funding from our university). We placed electronic banner ads in three online publications of *Tricycle* and print ads in the magazines *Buddhadharma, Shambala Sun,* and *Tricycle.* Partly because the electronic means

of communication appeared earlier, and therefore some potential survey respondents who saw the print ads had already done the survey, we found the electronic means of communication much more effective in generating respondents. For every dollar spent on electronic ads and free e-mail invitations, we got twenty-nine respondents; once the paid advertisements appeared in print, we received only one respondent for each dollar spent (Wiist et al. 2010). Moreover, because the e-mail invitations continued to circulate for the entire six-month period of data collection, those may still have been generating respondents even after the appearance of the print ads, so the figures may be even more in favor of electronic means—noteworthy for those aspiring to gather data through such a survey approach.

Our method resulted in 1,237 respondents who completed at least some of the survey, and with Buddhist practices as the first section, we have our most complete data here; a few others visited the site but did not answer any questions. Only 775 completed the entire survey; we hypothesize that this drop-off in respondents throughout the survey was because of loss of interest, or survey fatigue, or technical problems such as having the server "time-out" after an hour. Our survey is a convenience sample of English-speaking Buddhist practitioners with access to an internet connection. Responses came from all continents, but this article presents findings regarding those who responded from North America and Europe. Some respondents did not answer all questions, so on the questions discussed here the average number of respondents is 718 people. The findings presented here focus on the practices of these contemporary Western Buddhists; see the Appendix for the thirty-four questions discussed here.

For our respondents, forty-seven is the median age, 58 percent of them are female, and they are very highly educated. Some 31 percent graduated college, and an astounding 50 percent say that they have earned an advanced degree (doctorate, master's degree, or professional school degree) beyond college! Our survey found that 90 percent of respondents describe themselves as white or Caucasian.

Of these contemporary Western Buddhist practitioners, 72 percent answered "I am a Buddhist," with only a dozen respondents saying that they were born into Buddhist families (questions 1 and 2 on our survey). We were interested to know the prevalence of the tradition of taking the Three Refuges to mark membership in Buddhism: 63 percent said that they had done this formally before other Buddhists, another 11 percent had made the pronouncement informally or privately, and another 10 percent had not pronounced this formula, but regard themselves as Buddhists (question 3). Adding these responses together produces 84 percent who say that they regard themselves as Buddhists on this question (though question 1 had produced only 72 percent who placed themselves in the category "I am a Buddhist"). The mean length of time engaged in Buddhist practice was eleven and a half years.

Various researchers have noted a tendency in the current era for people to maintain affiliations with two or even more religious and/or spiritual traditions. Goosen (2007), in an empirical study of adults in Sydney, Australia, found "dual religious belonging" to be widespread, found Buddhism to be particularly tolerant of such an approach, and concluded that his data showed a pattern of "adherence to one main religion while having a second religion on which the individual draws" (159). Our survey also demonstrates the presence of "dual religious identity," but only to a limited extent in this group of contemporary Buddhist practitioners. Over 79 percent of our respondents are not members of other religions (see question 6). Of those who are the most frequently cited other religions in which they participate are as follows:

1. Unitarian Universalist (thirty people of 148 who answered "yes")
2. Mainstream Protestant (27)
3. Catholicism (26)
4. Judaism (20)
5. Hinduism (17)
6. Pagan/Wicca/New Age (16)

Our survey did not find very many people casually or vaguely interested in Buddhism, the sort of people Thomas Tweed (1999) calls "nightstand Buddhists." They exist, of course; not many such people completed our survey, however, and we hypothesize that only those with a keen interest in Buddhism would be sufficiently dedicated to complete the long survey. Half our respondents (50.9 percent) say that they "attend religious services at a temple with one or more Buddhist priests." Our respondents describe themselves as dedicated practitioners: 93 percent say that they read and study Buddhist scriptures (question 13). Some 64 percent say that they are now exclusively participating in one Buddhist tradition; the most frequently listed are

1. Tibetan (51 percent of those answering that they participate in one tradition)
2. Zen (or Ch'an or Sōn = 25 percent)

To the question (number 18), "Have you been formally instructed in Buddhist doctrines and ideas by a Buddhist monk or nun in a temple, church, lecture, or meditation hall setting?" the vast majority (80 percent) said "yes." An even higher percentage, 98.5 percent, said that they had received Buddhist teachings from recordings and/or books (question 19).

Our data highlight the difficulty of counting the number of contemporary Western Buddhists. Indeed, even the question concerning how many Buddhists there are in the United States is much contested, partly because the U.S. Census does not include questions on religion that would allow respondents to describe at least the one religious tradition with which they identify most strongly. As a result, scholars make estimates that differ sharply. For example, the estimate for the mid-1990s by Baumann (1997) is 1.6 percent of the population, while the Pew Forum's "U.S. Religious Landscape Survey" (2008) states that it found only 0.7 percent.[3] Wuthnow and Cadge (2004: 365) provide an extensive range as their estimate: "In the total adult population of approximately 209 million, these figures suggest that between 0.07 percent and 1.9 percent of the public might be sufficiently affiliated with Buddhism to qualify as Buddhists." (Their numbers indicate, in fact, 0.7 percent as the lower end of the estimate, so the stated figure is a typographic error.) Gregory (2001: 237) cites a figure of "between 0.5 percent and 1.5 percent of the total population." A Buddhist website estimates that 2 percent of the U.S. population is Buddhist (http://www.thedhamma.com/buddhists_in_the_world.htm). Ostrowski (2006) uses figures from this website by the Vipassana Foundation to support the idea that there are "nearly six million Buddhists in the United States" (which would be about 2 percent of the total population).[4] Self-identification as Buddhist still seems the most reliable method of enumerating the population, so our survey explores this feature of our respondents.

Our survey supplies some data on the issue concerning how Buddhist practitioners in North America and Europe describe themselves in relation to Buddhism. The question how contemporary Western Buddhist practitioners define being a "Buddhist" and the related question how scholars should define a "Buddhist" was first raised by Charles Prebish (1979: 188–189). He clearly endorses acceptance of the practitioner's own affirmation "I am a Buddhist" as definitive. Our respondents, however, include a substantial number who engage in Buddhist practices but do not identify themselves as Buddhists.

One of the most striking features of our Buddhist practitioners is their dedication to the practice of meditation: 98 percent say that they meditate, 61 percent once or more per day. This can be compared with the similar findings of a 2006 survey in Berlin (Prohl and Rakow 2008: 14–15), which showed that 97 percent of their respondents rated meditation as "important" or "very important" in their activity in Buddhism. Similarly, 92 percent of Coleman's respondents ranked meditation first in importance over ritual activity and social relationships with other members (Coleman 2001: 119–120). For our respondents, the mean duration of a typical meditation session is forty-four minutes (with standard deviation = 50). Over 76 percent said that they had received meditation instruction from a monk or nun. Almost 94 percent said that they had been instructed by writings or recordings of modern meditation teachers. We were interested to have the respondents be specific about their practice of meditation, to identify what they do when engaged in meditation practice. In their discussion of earlier studies of meditation, Lee and Newberg (2005: 457) observed:

> Unfortunately, many studies did not specify or describe the type of meditation used. A wide variety of methods may be used, including some in which the body is immobile (Zazen, Vipassana), others in which the body is let free (Siddha Yoga, the Latihan, the chaotic meditation of Rajneesh), and still others in which the person participates in daily activities while meditating (Mahamudra, Shikan Taza, Gurdjieff's 'self-remembering'). So it is not clear which forms are beneficial and what aspects of meditation are providing the benefits.

When we asked what forms of meditation they engaged in, and provided an array of possible choices in an effort to be more specific about

what "meditation" might mean to practitioners, we got the following results. The most frequently cited types of meditation are
1. noticing the breath without counting (370 respondents)[5]
2. mindfulness (324)
3. mantra recitation (290)
4. cultivation of loving-kindness (273)

With regard to meditation, perhaps the most surprising finding is that 65 percent said that they had completed a formal retreat or stayed in a monastery for intensive practice of meditation. Yet only 39 percent say that they have completed a course in meditation (such as Vipassana or Insight meditation).

Our respondents answered (questions 27–30) that they often or very often are engaged in "Buddhist practice that includes conscious efforts to increase your altruism and compassion" (88 percent marking 4 or 5 on the five-point scale). They answered with equal frequency that they are engaged in "Buddhist practice that includes conscious efforts to increase your loving-kindness" (88 percent). These are the first two of the traditional four Buddhist "sublime states" (brahma-vihāra), regarded by Buddhists as skillful ways of behaving. We also asked how often these Buddhist practitioners were engaged in "Buddhist practice that includes conscious efforts to decrease your anger and/or hatred" (82 percent marking 4 or 5 on the five-point scale). They answered with equal frequency that they are engaged in "Buddhist practice that includes conscious efforts to decrease your attachment and/or greed" (82 percent). These findings reflect traditional Buddhist meditative practices.

We also asked a question on each element of the Eightfold Path, seeking to determine the respondents' perception of their understanding and ability to practice each one (see question 34 in the Appendix). Responses were recorded on a five-point scale ranging from "no understanding" to the top two categories of "understand and can easily apply in daily life" and "understand and can teach to others." Below are shown the combined percentage of responses in the top two categories of greatest understanding and ability to practice:
1. Right understanding = 52 percent
2. Right thought = 54 percent
3. Right speech = 58 percent
4. Right action = 62 percent

5. Right livelihood = 71 percent
6. Right effort = 56 percent
7. Right mindfulness = 57 percent
8. Right concentration = 49 percent

Considering that in seven of the eight components, the majority of respondents say that they understand, can practice, and many can also teach that aspect of the Path; we have a group of confident practitioners who regard themselves as quite capable.

The design of our survey involved data collection though a website that was available for six months. Respondents could complete the survey at a time convenient to them and at no cost. Partly as a consequence of this design, and despite its great length, our survey appears to be the largest ever done on Buddhist practitioners.[6]

Discussion

The demographic profile of our survey respondents is similar to that of earlier surveys of Buddhists in the Western world. Very similar to our findings are those of Coleman's large survey of 359 U.S. Buddhists: his respondents were 58 percent female, and 32 percent had college degrees, with another 51 percent holding advanced degrees beyond college (Coleman 2008: 192–193). Our survey had a female majority, as does the survey in Germany by Prohl and Rakow (2008: 8), in which 52 percent were female. These findings contrast in all respects with a recent attempt at a representative survey, the Pew Forum, that found a population of Buddhists in the United States that was 53 percent male, and in which only 26 percent had a postgraduate education, so the Pew respondents are a much less well-educated group than we found. Our survey's findings are also very similar to those of Coleman (2008: 192–193) with regard to race, but quite different from the Pew survey's 53 percent white respondents; both these surveys were conducted only in the United States.

Clearly, the North American and European respondents in our survey are Buddhist practitioners who, to a great degree, are "convert" Buddhists rather than "cradle" or "birthright" Buddhists, i.e., they have chosen to engage in Buddhist practices rather than inheriting the tradition of engaging in Buddhist practices from their families. That contemporary Buddhism in the Western world has this duality has long been noted, indeed, some scholars have referred to "two Buddhisms" existing in the

West, or two separate lines of development.⁷ In light of the fact that for many of our respondents there may have been no dramatic, transformative experience causing a formal change in religious affiliation, perhaps "Buddhist by choice" rather than "Buddhist by conversion" should be the terminology. Of course, neither of these groups is monolithic, and both groups are becoming more diverse. "Convert" Buddhism (or "Buddhists by choice") seems to be increasingly diverse ethnically, and "cradle" Buddhism includes both recent immigrants from Asia and people of Asian heritage who have resided for generations outside Asia. Children of "convert" Buddhists would be "cradle" Buddhists, by definition. Some people in each group are biracial or multiracial, also. An example of this change is that the Buddhist Churches of America organization has in recent decades become more ethnically diverse, has ceased to be exclusively Japanese, and conducts services in English (Tanaka 2007). In an effort to have our survey represent the full spectrum of Buddhist practitioners, we directly contacted major Buddhist organizations in the Western world that have considerable ethnic diversity. Despite our outreach efforts, the sample of respondents in our survey does not reflect the ethnic diversity of Buddhism in North America and Europe. This outcome is likely because of the data-gathering method employed: the Internet and advertisements in magazines with a largely Caucasian readership. A study in the United States by Ostrowski (2006: 97) indicated that "the profile of those using the Internet to access information on Buddhism tended to be white (72 percent)," suggesting that Asian-American Buddhists make less use of the internet regarding Buddhism, and thus may not have been as well represented in our survey as a consequence.

Our survey depicts contemporary Western Buddhism as having a female majority. Indeed, as observed by Coleman (2008: 190–191),

> No other change is more important to Western Buddhism than the way it is redefining gender. ... nearly all the Western Buddhist groups recognize the full equality of the sexes and the ability of anyone of either gender to realize his or her true nature and attain enlightenment.

That the majority of respondents are female not only in our survey but also in the surveys by Coleman (2001) and Prohl and Rakow (2008) suggests that women find contemporary Western Buddhism a congenial environment.

The four hypotheses presented at the outset of this article that guided formulation of the questions for the survey are all supported by the data we collected.

Hypothesis (1): Contemporary Western Buddhist practitioners are more likely to identify themselves as Buddhist than as members of other religious traditions, and to have marked that identity in a formal way such as pronouncing the Three Refuges formula. As indicated above, the great majority of our respondents say that they identify with Buddhism, and they have marked this by pronouncing the Three Refuges formula (72–84 percent). Some who have not done so identify themselves as Buddhists as well. While the Three Refuges formula is widely used in Theravāda and Tibetan Buddhist traditions, it is not in Zen, for example.

Hypothesis (2): Contemporary Western Buddhist practitioners are more likely to engage in meditation than to attend Buddhist religious services supervised by clergy. Only about half (50.9 percent) of our respondents attend religious services at a temple with one or more priests, while 98 percent engage in meditation practice.

Hypothesis (3): Contemporary Western Buddhist practitioners who engage in meditation are more likely to engage in a variety of meditative practices, practices that they regard as identifiably distinct, than to engage in a single meditative technique. Our respondents engage in multiple different techniques under the heading of "meditation," an average of four different techniques (4.06 techniques per practitioner per week).

Hypothesis (4): Buddhist practitioners today engage in conscious efforts to increase loving-kindness and compassion through meditation practices. This and the preceding hypothesis highlight the point that Buddhist meditation is an array of techniques, with particular ones designed to overcome particular hindrances (such as anger or greed) or to cultivate particular virtues or beneficial states (such as loving-kindness or compassion).

Our questions on the first two of the traditional four Buddhist *brahmavihara*, "sublime states" regarded by Buddhists as skillful ways of behaving, produced the fascinating response from 88 percent of practitioners that they are engaged in conscious efforts through their practices to increase their loving-kindness, compassion, and altruism. While these qualities are often regarded in Western cultures as innate moral attributes, the Buddhist tradition regards them as skillful behaviors and attitudes that can be learned. Loving-kindness, compassion, and altruism are deliberately and systematically cultivated through Buddhist meditation, and the same techniques diminish the unskillful behaviors and attitudes of anger, hatred, attachment, and greed. Loving-kindness (*metta* in Pali; *maitri* in Sanskrit) is the first of the four *brahma-vihara*; compassion (*karunā*) is the second. With the other two (sympathetic joy and equanimity), these four Buddhist virtues are often presented in Buddhist scriptures and modern teachings.

One of the classic early discussions of the four *brahma-vihara* states is found in the "Tevijja Sutta" (*Digha Nikaya* 13.76–81). This early Buddhist scripture from the Pali Canon presents the Buddha persuading two brahmins that they should cultivate loving-kindness, compassion, sympathetic joy, and equanimity as means to attain the highest goal, here called liberation of the mind. A commentary on the Buddha's teachings, *Visuddhimagga* (or "The Path of Purification") by the fifth-century monk Buddhaghosa, devotes a chapter to the four *brahma-vihara* as subjects of meditation. As summarized by Gombrich (2009: 89), "Buddhaghosa is bypassing the problem of exactly what role the four divine states play in the spiritual development of an ordinary practitioner and saying that for a Buddha they are fundamental." Indeed, another early canonical text, the "Metta Sutta" (or "Karanīya Metta Sutta" from *Sutta Nipata* 1.8), presents the idea that cultivation of loving-kindness alone leads to nirvana. These early Buddhist texts are the basis for the argument by Gombrich (1998, 2009: 75–91) that in early Buddhism, loving-kindness and compassion are means to the attainment of nirvana.

Modern teachers also have cited the importance of systematic cultivation of these states, and the corresponding reduction in the unskillful states such as anger and hatred. An introduction to the practice of Buddhist meditation by British Buddhist teacher Kamalashila (1996) devotes a chapter to loving-kindness meditation, describing the traditional technique of cultivating this attitude of "friendliness" first for oneself, then for a loved one, a neutral person, an enemy, and finally for all without distinction. Master Hsing Yun (1999: 99–101) presents contemplation on compassion as the means to overcome anger. The Dalai Lama (2001: 91) makes the following statement:

> Compassion is the wish that others be free of suffering. It is by means of compassion that we aspire to attain enlightenment. It is compassion that inspires us to engage in the virtuous practices that lead to Buddhahood. We must therefore devote ourselves to developing compassion.

Of particular import in this regard is the statement by the Dalai Lama with which this article began, describing love and compassion as producing both religious benefits and the worldly benefits of good physical and mental health (see also Davidson and Harrington 2001). Thich Nhat Hanh (1996: 40–41) observes, "I have to deal with my anger with care, with love, with tenderness, with non-violence." This is so, he says, because anger is part of oneself, and meditation is "first of all to produce awareness of anger," to gain insight into how anger arises from ignorance. These modern teachers, representing the full range of Buddhist traditions, and well known among Western Buddhists, affirm the fundamental place of loving-kindness and compassion in meditative practice and the benefits of cultivating these states.

Also noteworthy with regard to the strong commitment to meditation practice in our respondents is a striking feature of contemporary Western Buddhism, the prevalence of practitioners who lie somewhere between the traditional roles of monastic and lay follower. Wetzel (2002: 282) has observed that the lifestyle of contemporary Western Buddhist practitioners results in "people who are neither monks nor nuns, neither priests nor part of a religious structure, and yet are full-time practitioners who teach secular Buddhism in a secular setting." Coleman (2008: 188–189) too has drawn attention to the innovative approach in the West: "Not really monks, but far more involved and dedicated than most lay people, Western practitioners are hard to classify with categories their teachers imported from Asia." Indeed, in our survey, 3.6 percent describe themselves as monks or nuns, and 1.8 percent of our respondents say that they are not formally ordained but live like monks or nuns. The practices of contemporary Western Buddhists constitute a new paradigm and merit further study.

Buddhist meditation is clearly central to the lives of contemporary Western Buddhist practitioners who responded to our survey, the feature of Buddhism with which virtually every one of them is engaged. One might regard meditation practice as largely private and individualistic in nature, the definitive practice of privatized religion. As Tweed comments in his article "Why are Buddhists So Nice?" (2008: 91),

> ... Buddhism has been interpreted as individualistic and pacifist and in harmony with shared cultural values ... (and) this image of the solitary meditator ... seems to resonate with long-standing American affirmations of individualism, the inclination to celebrate the value and authority of the individual, not the church or the state.

He also observes that such an image is, of course, not the complete picture of Buddhism.

While "religiousness" or the extent of a person's commitment to practice has typically been measured in terms of attendance at religious services (Hall, Meador, & Koenig, 2008), this may not be the best measure for a small religious minority that is relatively recently established. Our respondents are about twice as likely to engage in meditation as to attend religious services presided over by clergy. It is also true, however, that meditation is typically learned in a group context. Engaging in meditation should not be regarded as a solitary endeavor; there is a social dimension. Our respondents indicate that they often attend meditation sessions with others, have learned to meditate from teachers, and attend intensive meditation retreat sessions—all of which are group activities rather than private or individualistic practices. Our respondents indicate that they engage in practices to increase their compassion and/or altruism, and their loving-kindness, qualities that one brings to fruition in relation to others. The fact that meditation is a key component of contemporary Western Buddhist practice does not make its practitioners isolated individuals.

Research on contemporary Western Buddhism is in its infancy, and this survey is one data set that contributes toward our understanding of what Buddhism is becoming outside of Asia. This survey shows the centrality of meditation in the lives of contemporary Western Buddhist practitioners, who place a special emphasis on cultivation of loving-kindness and compassion in their practices for healing emotional states deemed not beneficial. The method we employed could be utilized in other studies of Buddhists, or members of other religious traditions. We extend our work into new areas and look forward to additional work being done to shed light on contemporary Western Buddhism.

Works cited

Baumann, Martin, 1997, "The Dharma Has Come West: A Survey of Recent Studies and Sources," *Journal of Buddhist Ethics* 4, pp. 194–211.

Coleman, James W., 2001, *The New Buddhism: The Western Transformation of an Ancient Tradition*, New York: Oxford University Press.

Coleman, James W., 2008, "The Emergence of a New Buddhism: Continuity and Change," in Paul David Numrich, ed., *North American Buddhists in Social Context*, Leiden: Brill, pp. 195–201.

Dalai Lama, 2001, *An Open Heart: Practicing Compassion in Everyday Life*, ed. Nicholas Vreeland. New York: Little Brown & Co.

Dalai Lama, 2005, *How to Expand Love: Widening the Circle of Loving Relationships*. Translated and edited by Jeffrey Hopkins. New York: Atria Books.

Davidson, R. J, and A. Harrington, eds., 2001, *Visions of Compassion: Western Scientists and Tibetan Buddhists Examine Human Nature*, New York: Oxford University Press.

Gombrich, R. F., 1998, *Kindness and Compassion as Means to Nirvana*, Gonda Lecture Series. Amsterdam: Royal Netherlands Academy of Arts and Sciences.

Gombrich, R. F., 2009, *What the Buddha Thought*, London: Equinox.

Goosen, Gideon, 2007, "An Empirical Study of Dual Religious Belonging," *Journal of Empirical Theology* 20(2), pp. 159–78.

Gregory, Peter N., 2001, "Describing the Elephant: Buddhism in America," *Religion and American Culture* 11(2), pp. 233–63.

Hall, D. E., K. G. Meador, and H. G. Koenig, 2008, "Measuring Religiousness in Health Research: Review and Critique," *Journal of Religion and Health* 47, pp. 134–63.

Kamalashila, 1996, *Meditation: The Buddhist Way of Tranquillity and Insight*, 2nd ed, Birmingham, UK: Windhorse.

Koenig, H.G., M.E. McCullough, and D.B. Larson, 2001, *Handbook of Religion and Health*, New York: Oxford University Press.

Lee, B.Y., and A.B. Newberg, 2005, "Religion and Health: A Review and Critical Analysis," *Zygon: Journal of Religion & Science* 40.2, pp. 443–68.

Machachek, D.W., 1999, "The Appeal of Soka Gakkai in the United States: Emergent Transmodernism," *Research in the Social Scientific Study of Religion* 10, pp. 57–75.

Marks, L., 2005, "Religion and Bio-psycho-social Health: A Review and Conceptual Model," *Journal of Religion and Health* 44, pp. 173–86.

McLellan, Janet, 2008, "Themes and Issues in the Study of North American Buddhists and Buddhism," in Paul David Numrich, ed., *North American Buddhists in Social Context*, Leiden: Brill, pp. 19–49.

Nhat Hanh, Thich, 1996, *Being Peace*, Berkeley, CA: Parallax Press, First ed. 1987.

Numrich, Paul David, 1996, *Old Wisdom in the New World. Americanization in Two Immigrant Theravada Buddhist Temples*, Knoxville: University of Tennessee Press.

Numrich, Paul David, 2003, "Two Buddhisms Further Considered," *Contemporary Buddhism* 4.1, pp. 55–78.

Ostrowski, Ally, 2006, "Buddha Browsing: American Buddhism and the Internet," *Contemporary Buddhism* 7.1, pp. 91–103.

Pew Forum on Religion & Public Life, 2008, "*U.S. Religious Landscape Survey*" http://religions.pewforum.org/ (accessed on December 29, 2009).

Prebish, Charles S., 1979, *American Buddhism*, North Scituate, MA: Duxbury Press.

Prebish, Charles S., 1993, "Two Buddhisms Reconsidered," *Buddhist Studies Review* 10.2, pp. 187–206.

Prohl, Inken, and Katja Rakow, 2008, "Transformationen buddhistisch inspirierter Vorstellungen und Praktiken: Eine empirische Studie im Raum Berlin," *Transformierte Buddhismen* 1, pp. 3–27.

Tanaka, Kenneth K., 2007, "The Individual in Relation to the Sangha in American Buddhism: An Examination of 'Privatized Religion'," *Buddhist-Christian Studies* 27, pp. 115–27.

Tweed, Thomas, 1999, "Night-Stand Buddhists and Other Creatures: Sympathizers, Adherents, and the Study of Religion," in D. Williams, and C. Queen, ed., *American Buddhism: Methods and Findings in Recent Scholarship*, Richmond, UK: Curzon, pp. 71–90.

Tweed, Thomas, 2008, "Why Are Buddhists So Nice? Media Representations of Buddhism and Islam in the United States Since 1945," *Material Religion* 4.1, pp. 91–93.

Wetzel, Sylvia, 2002, "Neither Monk nor Nun: Western Buddhists as Full-Time Practitioners," in C. Prebish, and M. Baumann, eds., *Westward Dharma: Buddhism Beyond Asia*, Berkeley: University of California Press, pp. 275–84.

Wiist, W.H., B. Sullivan, H. Wayment, and M. Warren, 2010, "A Web-based Survey on the Relationship between Buddhist Practices, Health, and Psychological Characteristics: Research Methodology and Preliminary Results," *Journal of Religion & Health*, 49(1), pp. 18–31.

Wilson, Jeff, 2008, "'Deeply Female and Universally Human': The Rise of Kuan-Yin Worship in America," *Journal of Contemporary Religion* 23.3, pp. 285–306.

Wuthnow, R., and W. Cadge, 2004, "Buddhists and Buddhism in the United States: The Scope of Influence," *Journal for the Scientific Study of Religion* 43, pp. 363–80.

Notes

1. The data presented in this article are part of a larger survey conducted by an interdisciplinary team of researchers, including faculty members from Religious Studies, Health Sciences, and Psychology at Northern Arizona University. I thank Meghan Warren (Assistant Professor in Health and Human Services, Northern Arizona University) for help with the data. The survey includes a large number of questions on health, diet, and psychological characteristics in addition to Buddhist practices and represents an effort to diversify the growing body of research on health, healing, and religion/spirituality. As noted by recent reviews of research in this field (Hall, Meador, & Koenig, 2008; Koenig, McCullough, & Larson, 2001; Marks 2005), most of the published research on religion, health, and healing has involved studies of Protestant Christians. Our findings are forthcoming in a series of publications, the first of which is Wiist et al. (2010).
2. McLellan (2008: 20). In a similar vein, Wuthnow and Cadge (2004: 364) observed "…nobody knows precisely how many people there are in the United States who practice aspects of Buddhism and/or consider themselves Buddhists, and thus it is impossible to establish precisely just how much Buddhism or the broader cultural influences of Buddhism may have grown."
3. The Pew Forum on Religion & Public Life released its "U.S. Religious Landscape Survey" (http://religions.pewforum.org) in January 2008. Pew's figures on the number of Buddhists interviewed are inconsistent, however. The methodology section shows a total of 35,957 interviewees, 411 identifying themselves as Buddhists. Yet the stated percentage of Buddhists in the United States is 0.7 percent. If this percentage is correct, they interviewed only 252 Buddhists; if the total of 411 interviewed is correct, then Buddhists are 1.1 percent of the U.S. population they interviewed.
4. Ostrowski (2006: 91) also inexplicably states that "Despite this seemingly large number of adherents, American Buddhists comprises (sic) only 3.6 percent of the 1.5 billion total Buddhist population worldwide (Vipassana Foundation 2006)." Where the figure of 3.6 percent of 1.5 billion to be accurate, the United States would have 54 million Buddhists, which certainly is not the case.
5. Respondents were allowed to select more than one category in this question to describe how they meditate.
6. As noted earlier, Pew may have interviewed as many as 411 Buddhists, though there is some ambiguity. The survey by Coleman (2001: 10) was a "purposive sample" of 359 respondents at seven Buddhist centers (two Tibetan, two Zen, two Vipassana, and one unaffiliated). Machachek's (1999) survey of Soka Gakkai Buddhism in the United States included 401 respondents. Prohl and Rakow (2008: 8) had 224 respondents in Berlin.
7. The first to call attention to the "two Buddhisms" is Charles Prebish (1979: 51); see also 1993. Numrich (1996) refers to "parallel congregations" to highlight the existence of "dichotomous groups" of Asian immigrants and American converts; his 2003 article provides an historical overview of scholarship on the issue. Wilson (2008: 287) uses the terms "birthright Buddhists" and "cultural Buddhists" to refer to Asian-American Buddhists.

Appendix: Buddhist Health Study Questions on Buddhist Practices

1. In which of the following categories would you place yourself?
    - I am a Buddhist.
    - I believe some aspects of Buddhism and/or I engage in some Buddhist practices.
2. Which category below best describes you?
    - Born into a Buddhist family
    - Converted to Buddhism
    - I believe and/or practice some aspects of Buddhism.
3. Have you taken the 3 Refuges to mark membership in Buddhism?
    - Yes, formally before other Buddhists
    - Yes, informally or privately
    - No, not formally but I regard myself as Buddhist.
    - No, but I believe and/or practice some aspects of Buddhism.
4. Which of the following categories best describes you?
    - I am an officially ordained monk or nun.
    - I am a lay follower.
    - I live as a monk, nun, or priest, but am not officially ordained.
    - I believe and/or practice some aspects of Buddhism.
5. Which of the following categories best describes you?
    - I regularly attend meetings of a Buddhist sangha or church.
    - I regularly attend meetings of a Buddhist meditation group.
    - I occasionally attend meetings of Buddhist groups.
    - I am a solitary Buddhist practitioner.
6. In addition to being a Buddhist or practicing some aspects of Buddhism, are you also a participating member of another religious or spiritual tradition?
    - Yes
    - No

If yes → Which one(s)? Click all that apply:
   - Jewish
   - Catholic
   - Mainstream Protestant (Episcopalian, Methodist, Baptist, etc.)
   - Unitarian Universalist
   - New Thought (Unity Church, etc.)
   - Other: _____

If yes → How well accepted are your Buddhist identity and practices in this tradition?

Not at all				Very well
•	•	•	•	•

7. For how long have you been practicing Buddhism?
    _____ months _____ years
8. Are other members of your family Buddhists?
    - Yes
    - No

If yes → Which of those below? (click all that apply)
- Spouse
- Child(ren)
- Grandchild(ren)
- Parent(s)
- Other relatives

9. Do you attend religious services at a temple with one or more Buddhist priests?
   - Yes
   - No

If yes → How often?

    Almost never   Very often

    •   •   •   •   •

10. Have you attended a session of chanting of Buddhist scriptures as part of a regular religious service?
    - Yes
    - No

11. Have you attended a session of chanting of Buddhist scriptures as part of a funeral ceremony?
    - Yes
    - No

12. Does chanting or repeating a *mantra* play a role as part of your Buddhist religious practice?
    - Yes
    - No

13. Do you read and study Buddhist scriptures?
    - Yes
    - No

If yes → How often?

    Almost never   Very often

    •   •   •   •   •

14. Do you read and study the writings of modern Buddhist teachers?
    - Yes
    - No

If yes → How often?

    Almost never   Very often

    •   •   •   •   •

15. Do you engage in prayer in a Buddhist context?
    - Yes
    - No

If yes → How often?

Almost never					Very often
•	•	•	•	•	

If yes → Where do you pray most often?
- At home
- In religious services at a temple
- Other _____

16. Do you engage in rituals for your ancestors?
- Yes
- No

If yes → How often?

Almost never					Very often
•	•	•	•	•	

17. Are you now exclusively a member of one Buddhist tradition?
- Yes
- No

If yes → Which tradition?
- Zen/Ch'an/Son
- Pure Land (Jodo, Jodo-shin, Buddhist Churches of America, etc.)
- Shingon
- Soka Gakkai/Nichiren
- Tibetan (Gelug, Sakya, etc.)
- Theravada (Sri Lankan, Thai, etc.)
- Vipassana (Insight meditation, S.N. Goenka, etc.)
- Other: _____

If no, or if in the past you were engaged with one or more other Buddhist groups →
Which of the following traditions have been the most important to you? *(click all that apply)*
- Zen/Ch'an/Son
- Pure Land (Jodo, Jodo-shin, Buddhist Churches of America, etc.)
- Shingon
- Soka Gakkai/Nichiren
- Tibetan (Gelug, Sakya, etc.)
- Theravada (Sri Lankan, Thai, etc.)
- Vipassana (Insight meditation, S.N. Goenka, etc.)
- Other: _____

18. Have you been formally instructed in Buddhist doctrines and ideas by a Buddhist monk or nun in a temple, church, lecture, or meditation hall setting?
- Yes
- No

If yes → Please name the Buddhist tradition: _____ (same menu as #17.)

19. Have you received Buddhist teachings from books or recordings?
    - Yes
    - No
20. Do you practice Buddhist meditation?
    - Yes
    - No

If yes → Please describe the frequency of your meditation sessions:
    - Less than once a day
    - Once or more per day

If "Less than once a day" → Please describe the frequency of your meditation sessions:
    - Almost never
    - Sporadic but not regular
    - Often but not daily

If "Once or more per day" → Please describe the frequency of your meditation sessions:
    - Once a day
    - Once on some days, more on others
    - Usually twice a day
    - Usually more than twice a day

If yes → Describe the duration of your typical meditation session:
_____ minutes _____ hours

If yes → How much of your time in meditation per week is spent in each of the following practices?

Counting breaths _____ minutes
Noticing breath without counting _____ minutes
Focus on nothing in particular _____ minutes
Visualization _____ minutes
Mindfulness _____ minutes
Calming (*shamatha*) _____ minutes
Insight (*vipassana*) _____ minutes
Loving-kindness (metta) _____ minutes
Contemplation of *koan* _____ minutes
Reciting a phrase (*mantra*) _____ minutes
Cultivating altruism (such as *tonglen*, "take & give") _____ minutes
Other practices _____ minutes

21. Have you received instruction in meditation from a monk or nun?
    - Yes
    - No
22. Have you received instruction in meditation from a teacher of meditation who was not a monk or nun (a lay follower)?
    - Yes
    - No
23. Have you received instruction in meditation from reading scriptures?
    - Yes
    - No

24. Have you received instruction in meditation from writings or recordings by modern meditation teachers?
    - Yes
    - No
25. Have you ever completed a formal retreat, or stayed in a monastery for an intensive practice of meditation?
    - Yes
    - No

If yes → How often have you done such a period of meditation?
    _____ time(s)

If yes → How many total days in the past year have you been in such an intensive meditation?
    _____ days

26. Have you ever completed a course in meditation (such as Vipassana or Insight meditation)?
    - Yes
    - No

If yes → How often have you done such a period of meditation?
    _____ time(s)

If yes → How many total days in the past year have you been in such an intensive meditation?
    _____ days

27. To what extent has your Buddhist practice included conscious efforts to increase your altruism and compassion?

    Almost   Very
    never   often
    •   •   •   •   •

28. To what extent has your Buddhist practice included conscious efforts to decrease your anger and/or hatred?

    Almost   Very
    never   often
    •   •   •   •   •

29. To what extent has your Buddhist practice included conscious efforts to increase your loving-kindness?

    Almost   Very
    never   often
    •   •   •   •   •

30. To what extent has your Buddhist practice included conscious efforts to decrease your attachment and/or greed?

    Almost   Very
    never   often
    •   •   •   •   •

31. Are you a member of any Buddhist socially engaged or non-sectarian organizations?
    - Yes
    - No

If yes → Which one below? (click all that apply)
    - Buddhist Peace Fellowship
    - Free Tibet
    - Friends of the Western Buddhist Order
    - International Network of Engaged Buddhists
    - Prison Dharma Network
    - Sakyadhita, the International Association of Buddhist Women
    - World Fellowship of Buddhists
    - Other: _____

32. If in the past 12 months you have participated in an activity (e.g., volunteered, attended a local meeting or conference) of any community service organization that is not specifically a Buddhist organization, indicate the type of organization in which you participated (click all that apply):
    - Environmental
    - Human rights
    - Peace
    - Hunger
    - Disaster relief
    - Health/medical
    - Hospice
    - Civic
    - Political
    - Religious
    - Other

33. If in the past 12 months you have made a financial contribution to any community service organization that is not specifically a Buddhist organization, indicate the type of organization to which you contributed (click all that apply):
    - Environmental
    - Human rights
    - Peace
    - Hunger
    - Disaster relief
    - Health/medical
    - Hospice
    - Civic
    - Political
    - Religious
    - Other

34. We are interested to know your evaluation of your understanding of Buddhism's Eightfold Path. Of course, one may be well aware of some features of the Path and less well aware of others. Please use the following categories to indicate the extent of your understanding of each component. Marking 1 indicates the least understanding; marking 5 indicates the greatest extent of understanding.

1 = No understanding
2 = Requires more study; still trying to understand
3 = Understand but have difficulty applying in daily life
4 = Understand and can easily apply in daily life
5 = Understand and can teach to others

a.	Right understanding	1	2	3	4	5
b.	Right thought	1	2	3	4	5
c.	Right speech	1	2	3	4	5
d.	Right action	1	2	3	4	5
e.	Right livelihood	1	2	3	4	5
f.	Right effort	1	2	3	4	5
g.	Right mindfulness	1	2	3	4	5
h.	Right concentration	1	2	3	4	5

RELIGION AND HIV/AIDS PREVENTION IN NIGERIA

Jude Aguwa

The spread of the human immunodeficiency virus in Africa has reached epic proportions, and the controversy over the use of condoms as a preventive measure has also escalated. In South Africa, 5.7 million of the nation's 50 million people are infected with HIV. In 2001, 5.8 percent of Nigeria's 140 million were infected with the virus.[1] In dealing with this problem, which has been described as the twenty-first plague, some faith-based organizations have denounced condom use based on their sexual ethical teachings, while government and other secular agencies that pursue preventive programs endorse it based on its proven efficacy. The issues involved in this controversy will be the focus of this article. These issues include the following topics: religious beliefs, marital fidelity, abstinence, and condom use. The purpose of this study is to examine how religious teachings and policies affect the implementation of preventive programs of governments and civil organizations that advocate the use of condoms as an essential ingredient of a comprehensive prevention program. Furthermore, the study hopes to provide some insight that can be helpful in fostering more effective collaboration between faith-based organizations on the one hand, and governments and social organizations on the other.

The roots of controversy

In the Western world, the thinking about AIDS as a death sentence has changed. This is as a result of the development of treatments that enable persons infected with the virus to operate normally and to live out their life span. Hence, HIV/AIDS is treated as a manageable chronic disease. In Africa, however, the "death sentence" picture about HIV/AIDS continues to dominate. In a country such as Nigeria, there is still limited availability of preventive and treatment programs. Furthermore, there has been an insignificant drop in the number of deaths from AIDS. The euphemisms for HIV/AIDS denoting wasting, disappearance, and death are still used, and their images continue to fuel sentiments of fear and confusion and encourage stigmatization of victims.

To change this death-sentence image in Africa, the spread of the virus must be contained and death from AIDS reduced. Government and social organizations involved in preventive and treatment programs advocate the use of condoms with the hope that especially youth can practice safe sex. On the contrary, some religious groups that are also involved in preventive programs condemn the use of condoms. According to religious views, especially in Catholicism, the condom is a form of contraception and so its use is viewed as immoral.[2] Second, the availability of condoms is viewed as a contributing factor in early initiation of sex for young people as well as encouragement of extramarital sex.

The position taken by some religious groups with respect to condom use has been seen as subversive, myopic, and unrealistic. In a recent study involving four hundred and forty-three people, mostly young university students, half of them agree that the Catholic Church's teaching on contraceptives and condom use limits the effectiveness of preventing the spread of HIV.[3] An eminent Nigerian medical practitioner had expressed grave concerns on what amounted to a negative impact of religion:

> The steps being taken by all the governments of West Africa are basically along the ones that medical practice normally follows: prevention, treatments and rehabilitation. In terms of prevention, we are trying to change the sexual practices of the people. You have heard of ABC. ABC is a rational approach. A: Abstinence, B: Being faithful to one's partner and, of course, C: use of condoms in situations where those two are not possible. It's unfortunate that some people have brought religion into the whole thing. We are talking about the life and the death of people and we need to

be practical about it and actually accept that the three approaches are important.[4]

Other authors such as Chinyere Okunna and Ifeoma Dunu have also indicted religion with a negative appraisal of its role in the battle against HIV/AIDS. Sadly, there are clear indications that although religion seems to show sympathy for people living with HIV/AIDS (PPLWHA), it has blindly and steadfastly continued to refuse to fully accept the reality of preventing the spread of the virus through openness, advocacy, and awareness. In this regard, the role of religion is limited and religion undermines the effectiveness of combating the pandemic by stakeholders, including the media.[5]

Similarly, Irene Ogbogu and Omokhudu Idogo have pointed out that some of the policies of faith-based organizations "hinder efforts to promote safe sex and positive living…"[6]

It would appear that until a vaccine against the HIV/AIDS is developed, preventive programs championed by public and private organizations, governments, and faith-based groups will need to work side by side in the fight against the virus. If the various agencies, both secular and religious, worked collaboratively, the goal would more easily be achieved. This is why accusations that the views espoused in some religious sexual ethics in Africa are subversive deserve critical attention. A cursory history of Nigeria's HIV/AIDS experience will help focus the attention.

History: from denial to policy

The first report of HIV infection in Nigeria was in 1986. Until then, public knowledge about the ways the virus is passed from one person to another was based on rumor and speculation. Such rumors attributed HIV/AIDS to behaviors such as bestiality, homosexuality, and sexual promiscuity. Those who commit such acts offend God and could be severely punished. Such a conclusion is congruous with beliefs of the indigenous religion, as well as Christianity and Islam. In Exodus (chapter 9), the fifth plague was the pestilence that destroyed all the animals that belonged to Egyptians. In 2 Samuel (24: 10ff), God sent pestilence that killed seventy thousand Israelites as punishment for King David's sin.[7] The idea that bugs could be divine punishment plays well into Nigeria's intense religiosity.

When the announcement therefore came that a young woman had became infected with the virus after a visit to the dentist, public opinion got a jolt. But despite the stream of factual or scientific information that followed the announcement, varying forms of religio-ethical interpretative versions persisted. The evidence that in this part of the world the virus was spread mostly through heterosexual sex did not easily lead to abandoning the myths about it. This is because generally sexually transmitted infections could be blamed on promiscuity, a reason for divine punishment.

Ten years after the public notice that HIV/AIDS had arrived in Nigeria, the majority of Nigerians were still in the dark regarding its social and health ramifications. The following description of the condition of an HIV/AIDS victim of the time is powerfully revelatory of the miserable state of individual and public awareness: "It was 1997 and, like many of her fellow Nigerians Jegede-Ekpe was ignorant of what it meant to be infected with HIV. Her country was still in denial about its growing epidemic, and the stigmatization of AIDS could sometimes be as deadly as the virus itself."[8]

It was during this period—1997—that Nigeria's HIV prevalence rate was rising astronomically. With incessant prodding from the United Nations Joint Programme on HIV/AIDS (UNAIDS) and non-governmental organizations urging action, the government no longer could ignore the reality and enormity of the health crisis. The government's initial response consisted of the creation of HIV- and AIDS-related policies and action programs. These included the National Policy on HIV/AIDS, the Nigerian Antiretroviral Program, and AIDS Emergency Action Plan.

The National AIDS policy aims at improving behavior change, treatment, and prevention of sexually transmitted infections and promotion of condom use within the context of abstinence and fidelity. Condoms are openly available throughout Nigeria, and government works with family health organizations to ensure an extensive distribution program. Condoms have also been made affordable for most people. Various organizations working with government, except the faith-based ones, are convinced it is necessary to strengthen the distribution of condoms as a vital preventive measure.

Presently, Nigeria's HIV/AIDS policy and programs include control, education, surveillance, testing, and antiretroviral distribution. The government's goal to establish HIV/AIDS center at each state capital as well as sub-distribution centers in other locations within the state has been consistently pursued. In collaboration with public, private, and non-profit agencies, including faith-based organizations, the government's goal is to create preventive and care opportunities, to expand them and make them available to everyone. Television programs, the press media, and billboards have been used to disseminate information about testing, prevention, and treatment centers. Expansion of test and treatment centers has been ongoing, and retroviral drugs are offered freely.

These government-based activities are periodically reported in publications of the Federal Ministry of Health.[9] The publications are intended not only to provide important educational materials, but also to show that government's programs are being brought to capacity for an effective control of the HIV/AIDS epidemic. However, the need for collaboration with all civil society organizations including the faith-based is essential. Historically, these groups have supplemented government healthcare efforts. The hospitals built by religious groups are numerous and some are located in rural and remote areas, thus bringing to the grassroots sometimes the only access to healthcare. The views of healthcare workers in the faith-based hospitals with regard to condom use are certainly influential in those communities. It would be useful to examine some major tributaries of faith-influence with regard to receptivity to secular preventive programs.

Some religious beliefs and practices

The Nigerian society is strongly permeated by religious influences of the indigenous religion, Christianity, and Islam. Their influences are different and affect different parts of the country. As we discuss models of influences from the three religions, we will be able to appreciate their potentials for impacting secular preventive programs. First of all, we will examine the idea of illness causation in the Nigerian indigenous religion. In the indigenous society, the causes of illness were often related to supernatural sources. There is belief in divine affliction, which means that those who are immoral or who break the laws established by the deities are punished with physical or mental illness. Witchcraft was another explanation for several forms of illness and suffering. A witch is an evil person whose evil intentions and activities can bring about illness to others. Many parts of Nigeria are replete with witchcraft accusations; and in recent times, child-witch accusations have risen to frightening proportions. There were also other forms of illness attributed to the anger of ancestors over descendants who renege on their ritual responsibilities toward those ancestors. There is also strong belief that sorcerers are people who can magically introduce disease-causing agents in the bodies of their enemies. They can put charms and other negative power substances on the path of the intended victim. Those so affected fall sick. Another source of illness was infringement on taboos, which are actions, words, and occurrences that are forbidden. Some of them concern very serious issues such as incest or murder or breaking the rules of a particular deity. The very breaking of the taboo, even in secret, incurs ritual pollution. The rite of purification is required to restore the individual back to health and wholeness.

These beliefs have been weakened as a result of modernization and education, but are not yet fully dead. In a recent survey of four hundred and forty-three Nigerians, mostly university students, forty-eight percent agreed that illness can result from divine affliction. Thirty-nine percent disagreed. When the question was applied to HIV/AIDS, only fifteen percent agreed that HIV/AIDS can result from divine affliction. This goes to show the change in understanding that has occurred as a result of efforts by government and private organizations to create the necessary awareness. Yet the effort must continue toward having everyone embrace scientific and medical knowledge about the disease. As long as indigenous beliefs regarding illness causation remain popular, they will continue to affect prevention programs.[10] It is therefore important that administrators of programs aimed at preventing and treating HIV/AIDS understand the possible correlations between these beliefs and the readiness of individuals to embrace preventive measures that are proven to work. Seminars and workshops aimed at exposing such dangerous religious beliefs and the practices they legitimize must become part of the educational and awareness-creating programs.

With regard to influence from Christianity, I would like to examine faith healing, which is a major preoccupation of many Christian churches. Faith healing requires belief in supernatural powers that cause illness and influence healing. Because there is no known cure for AIDS, it means that people living with HIV/AIDS at some point are inclined to seek divine cure at faith-healing churches and services.

The popularity of faith healing has a long history of existence in Nigeria. Some Christian churches are dedicated to healing practices that involve rituals and prayers. The prophets of those churches claim the power to discover the causes of illnesses. Some illnesses are blamed on evil spirits and their agents; others on the sinful life of the sufferers. Misfortunes and illness can result from actions that pre-exist the individual. As the prophets explain, a person could be made to pay for the evil conduct of one's ancestors. In these prophet churches, rituals of deliverance take several forms. The prophet ministers conduct healing rituals and prescribe other actions for the moral reform of the sufferer.

Some other Christian churches, such as the Pentecostal and Charismatic churches, practice healing and deliverance of the sick, and this is an essential part of their worship ritual. Often guided by a literal reading of biblical miracles, these churches proclaim cures by invoking the power of Christ. In the mainline churches, such as the Catholic and Anglicans, faith healing is referred to as healing ministry. Several priests of the Catholic Church in Nigeria have experimented with faith healing and holy water ministries and have won innumerable followers. Some ministries have survived and continued to draw a large following, and many members of such churches believe that their healers possess special charisms or gifts.

Faith healing could be a serious diversionary practice, especially when it involves Christian ministers who "destroy" witches. In recent years, this practice has earned national and international notoriety following the unprecedented occurrence of witchcraft accusations in Nigeria. The news media reporting on the practices has been characterized by code words that tend to instill fear. Examples of such words and phrases include references to "the witchcraft industry"[11]; the "war over witches"[12]; "Helen Akpabio: Hitting hard on witchcraft."[13] The resurgence of witchcraft accusations became such a critical problem in Akwa Ibom, one of the States of Southern Nigeria, that the state governor had to publicly denounce the Christian minister who practiced the inhuman rituals. The national media thus reported it: "In Akwa Ibom State, we have over 150 children who have been thrown into the streets by pastors who claim the children are into witchcraft. They even attempted to burn some children alive in the State. We have rescued children who have been almost burnt to death on the basis that they are into witchcraft."[14] Thus, the stigmatization of these supposed child witches is a consequence of the faith-healing therapeutic ritual of some Christian churches. In 2009, the government promulgated a law, making it a crime to accuse a child of witchcraft. It is of course true that civil laws do not easily resolve convictions based on faith and myths. The Indian caste system is a good example.

Christian faith-healing practice can bring about two types of influences that can affect HIV/AIDS prevention programs. First, it can take people's attention away from real practical and natural health resources. Furthermore, there are some people who do not have the sophistication to blend the specific nuances of healing and curing. As the saying goes, God heals, man cures. Second, the practice of faith healing can strengthen the tendency of blaming a person for the suffering. Most faith-healing practices tend to identify the cause of the suffering in personal moral flaws or in some action of angry supernatural powers. In most cases, the sufferer is made to accept some blame. As is well known, both in Nigeria and elsewhere, the blame game has featured very well in matters of HIV/AIDS and that has not really helped as a means of controlling the spread.

Finally, turning to Islam, we would like to discuss a type of religious influence that could be considered as supportive of prevention programs. The Muslim population of northern Nigeria has experienced lower prevalence of HIV/AIDS than the Christian population of the south. Islam is an enacted religion based on the *Sharia* and it has stringent laws on sexual morality and gender interactions. Claire Mark discussed some of these to explain the low rate of HIV/AIDS infection in the North. They include repression of Muslim women, non-use of alcohol by Muslims, and common practice of circumcision among Muslims.[15] Muslims, just as Christians and traditionalists, can blame the HIV/AIDS epidemic on sexual immoral behaviors that attract divine retribution. In Islam, however, divine retribution is not left totally in God's hands. Sins of sexual immorality are punished by Sharia law and not simply left to divine compassion as Christianity does. Muslims therefore are more likely to be deterred from premarital and extramarital affairs than Christians.

Considering the higher ratio of infection in the Christian south, that would appear to be a reasonable deduction.

These three religions maintain complex relationships with HIV/AIDS programs in Nigeria. The complexity is even more obvious with respect to the ABC program, for each of the religions speaks somewhat differently to the advocacy of marital fidelity, abstinence, and condom use. We will now explore the variances.

Marital fidelity: impact as preventive factor

While the Christian churches advocate monogamy, Islam and the indigenous Nigerian cultures permit polygamy. In the monogamous marriage, marital fidelity is expected to be observed by both spouses. In the polygamous marriage, the man has several wives and this can give marital fidelity a different meaning. Be that as it may, infidelity does occur in both forms of marriage. But in a polygamous marriage, more individuals would be exposed to the risk of sexually transmitted infections. There are well-known examples in Nigeria and other countries in Africa of entire harems that have perished from HIV/AIDS. Women in a polygamous marriage do not necessarily have shared commitments to each other, which would legally or mutually require the avoidance of behaviors, capable of affecting the other women in the marriage. It is also to be expected that polygamous relationships that involve several women can undermine adherence to even a conventional sense of marital fidelity because the man might not always be able to fulfill the sexual needs of all the women. A wealthy Nigerian who died a few years ago knew this so well that in his will, he specified DNA tests of all the children from his several wives to prove paternity. The children he had not fathered were to be excluded from the inheritance.

Many Christian couples seriously commit to the goal to remain faithful to each other and it can be said that the majority succeed. Thus, fidelity is an indispensable value for an effective HIV/AIDS preventive strategy. Christian teaching on marital fidelity draws appropriate attention to the needs of both spouses and it condemns casual sex. In the evangelization of indigenous culture, Christian teaching on fidelity has factored in the suppression of social practices that can expose persons to serious risk. One of such practices is wife inheritance which requires a man to take over the widow of a deceased brother.[16] This can create a polygamous situation if the inheritor was already married. But even more seriously, if the brother died of AIDS, the inherited widow could be HIV positive. Given that autopsies are not usually required and testing for HIV is an uncommon practice, wife inheritance could constitute serious health risks. So also would the practice of wife hospitality, by which a man would allow his wife to sexually entertain a visiting friend. Christian marriage excludes every romantic relationship with a third party. It assures safe sex when faithfully observed and should serve as a goal in cultural transformation, and the behavior change that is required for combating HIV/AIDS.

Preaching marital fidelity in Nigeria still faces a few obstacles. First, some people are interested in reviving indigenous cultural practices because they believe that those practices were unjustifiably suppressed by the missionaries or the colonial government. A good example would be polygamy. Second, there are several factors that may be economic, social, or psychological in nature, and that can make marital fidelity difficult to observe. For example, there are some spouses who leave the home for distant places and for long periods in search of work; or soldiers involved in military campaigns while their spouses stay home. The Benue state of Nigeria, which for years has had the highest rate of HIV/AIDS infection, is an intense activity area involving truckers and commercial sex. Various studies have suggested connections between these activities and the prevalence of HIV/AIDS. Such circumstances can put enormous pressure on marital fidelity. The Catechism of the Catholic Church admits this by declaring marriage as existing under the regime of sin. It explains that marriage is "always threatened by discord, a spirit of dominion, infidelity, jealousy, and conflicts..."[17] This can mean that marital fidelity is not always compelling. It also can mean that fear of infection may be so compromised by other factors that it fails to serve as a deterrent. These realities support the case for the condom option in situations where observance of marital fidelity is likely to fail.

Abstinence and condom use
In Nigeria's indigenous cultures, sexual abstinence is valued, and that value has been reinforced by Christian teaching about sexual morality, as well as Islamic chastity laws. The Catholic Church has, however, been

most vocal in advocating abstinence and condemning condom use, and its position in these matters has drawn global attention as well as criticism. A look at the Church's HIV/AIDS policy can reveal the grounds for its advocacy and opposition.

The HIV/AIDS policy of Catholic Bishops' Conference of Nigeria is spelled out as follows: promotion of premarital abstinence and marital fidelity; promotion of abstinence by HIV-positive spouses and individuals; expression of love by HIV sero-discordant couples through non-genital means; discouragement of the use of condoms but provision of accurate and factual information on its effectiveness, including the limits of such effectiveness; and promotion of natural family planning between married couples, which enhances human capacity for faithfulness.[18] These goals are based on the official teachings of the Catholic Church, which states that "every action which, whether in anticipation of the conjugal act, or in its accomplishment, or in the development of its natural consequences, proposes, whether as an end or as a means, to render procreation impossible is intrinsically evil."[19]

Now and again the teaching is reiterated by church officials. Pope Benedict XVI and his predecessor firmly advocate abstinence and marital fidelity as the only moral choices open to Christians with respect to HIV/AIDS prevention. Specifically on Africa, their statements amount to denunciation of programs that distribute condoms even if Africa's HIV/AIDS situation has reached a critical stage. Pope Benedict has insisted that the spread of HIV in Africa should be tackled through fidelity and abstinence and not by condom use. He further suggested that use of condoms could aggravate or increase the spread, thus angering many in the scientific community.[20] The pope's views were supported by some protestant and Russian Orthodox leaders.[21] In Nigeria, the bishops' conference expressed unflinching support for the pope, claiming empirical knowledge as to what works or not. Thus, Archbishop Onaiyekan, speaking on behalf of the bishops' conference, said: "What reduces infections is less casual sex, not more condoms... The condom distributors should listen to the truth coming not only from the pope and bishops, but even from impartial and serious scientific research."[22] The bishop does not mention what research he refers to as impartial. Be that as it may, most studies are in agreement on issues of the science and preventive efficacy of condom use. But they may disagree on the sociological question as to whether the availability of condoms would encourage sexual freedom especially among young teenagers.

It appears a legitimate assumption that such sexual freedom would result in early initiation and high frequency of sexual activity by young people. The availability of condoms could also encourage premarital and extramarital sex. The empirical facts to prove this may derive from many years of the church's mission in the communities. The argument that some people may never be so compelled by religious teaching and aspirations as to forgo the exercise of their sexual freedom is equally weighty. Those convinced about this, such as Moghalu, see abstinence alone a limited prevention program.[23] As he explained:

> This is why the "ABC" approaches—abstinence, be faithful and condoms—is the best approach to preventing the spread of HIV/AIDS. Emphasizing one of these three components to the exclusion of the others is not good public health policy. Let the churches and mosques play their role in prevention and treatment. And let the public authorities do their duty to safeguard public health. Neither should stand in the way of the other.[24]

The reduction of such ideological clash is at the heart of this study. It is important to bear in mind that the criticisms over the ban of condom reflect genuine anxiety over the rising numbers of new HIV infections. It is a situation that calls for urgent and reasonable approaches that employ all necessary measures that have been proven to work in making sex safe for people for whom abstinence is a failing option. In this vulnerable group are mostly young unmarried people, and the idea of a suitable prevention program is one that offers them wider choices that include but go beyond abstinence. In other words, the program should provide a full range of options for safe sex and behavior change.

Principle and praxis

At one point, a non-traditionalist view regarding condom use, especially for Africa, seemed to be gaining support among some Catholic Church officials. In 2006, it was reported that Cardinal Carlo Maria Martini, following a green signal from the Vatican, spoke out on condom use to halt the spread of AIDS and said the following:

> "We need to do everything possible to combat AIDS. Under certain conditions, the use of condoms is necessary. Those who are afflicted have an obligation to protect the other partner," he told the Italian weekly newsmagazine *L'Espresso*. At the same time, he emphasized that this was not a green light for the church to actively start distributing condoms.[25]

But subsequent official comments, such as the ones issued by Pope Benedict as stated above, restored the traditionalist views. Any advocacy for condom use, even in the direst situations, would fly in the face of the ethical principle, namely, that the end does not justify the means. In proposing a solution to the problem posed by the church's teaching with respect to an effective preventive healthcare practice, Moghalu explained:

> Whatever our personal or religious views about sex outside of marriage, the reality is that, while not everyone is on sexual autopilot, not all that wish to abstain succeed in that aspiration. To preserve their lives—and a chance for a possible latter-day spiritual conversion—they better use a condom. It may be expecting too much to ask faith-based organizations to actively encourage the use of condoms. But public health is a legitimate concern and responsibility of governments. They cannot—and should not—be expected to prevent condom use in order to promote religious doctrines.[26]

In other words, while not denying the church its right to teach its members, the church is expected to exercise that right in such ways that healthcare efforts by government and other social organizations are not undermined. Having primary healthcare responsibility for its citizens requires government to provide and expand every preventive measure that is known to work. In other words, the church should apply critical caution in presenting its teachings on condom use, so that its teachings do not become such a constraining force that they would prevent religious people, when left with no other option, from embracing a measure that their government provides and advocates as part of responsible public healthcare provision.

Studies show that the use of condom has become popular among students in Nigeria universities.[27] The students belong to religions that expound traditionalist views about sex outside of marriage. To have ignored the traditionalist views in this matter shows how far young people have become empowered with regard to making practical decisions in matters of safe sex. Of course, according to Ogbogu and Idogho, "young people are the primary target group in HIV prevention in Nigeria."[28] The popular use of condoms among students also shows the growing understanding that HIV/AIDS is not an unavoidable divine retribution, but is a communicable disease that can be prevented sometimes by applying commonsense measures. Furthermore, it can also mean that religious people who ignore the ban on condom use have come to terms with the view that to deal with Africa's HIV/AIDS crisis, teaching about safe sex with suggestions to use every available means will more effectively slow the spread of the virus.

Conclusion

One recent study carried out in the United States shows that sex education focused on encouraging children to remain abstinent can persuade a significant proportion to delay sexual activity.[29] It may be true, therefore, that availability of condoms inspires sexual freedom and consequently early and more frequent sexual activities. However, in this article, we have reviewed information to show that going by a universal experience, abstinence as a single preventive measure can fail woefully with regard to HIV/AIDS.

Public pronouncements by faith-based organizations opposing condom use will remain controversial in the present Nigerian situation. This is because the preventive program sponsored by government and some social organizations that include condom use seem to be succeeding. That success is reflected in the drop in Nigeria's HIV statistical report for the year 2008. Of course, other factors that may have contributed to the success cannot be ignored.

It is possible that this controversy between ideology and pragmatism can be reduced if the different groups reexamine their anthropological assumptions. The church's version of sexual morality, which upholds genuine and reasonable moral values and personal principles of discipline, is positively affirming of the human moral capacity, and points to the transcendent nature of human sexuality. But the absolute nature of this anthropology and the apparent inflexibility in its interpretation in matters such as just discussed may easily give the impression that people could be sacrificed on the altar of doctrines. A viable anthropology, whether secular or religious, that intends to be realistic should effectively speak to Africa's cultural, social, economic, and health issues and bring about desirable results. An inflexible traditionalist view could mean that the church will continue to face accusations of being out of touch with reality, when in fact the church, more than many other organizations, is immersed in people's real problems.

Notes
1. UNAIDS Report, 2008.
2. Catechism of the Catholic Church #2370.
3. Cf. Jude C. Aguwa, HIV/AIDS in Nigeria: study carried out in 2009 with the Olson Award Grant, Mercy College, NY.
4. Rose Ejembi, "Soon there'll be vaccine for AIDS" in *Daily Sun,* August 21, 2007. This statement is attributed to Professor Rogers Makanjuola, a psychiatrist at the Obafemi Awolowo University, Ile-Ife. At the time of publication he was the president of West African College of Physicians.
5. Chinyere Stella Okunna and Ifeoma Vivian Duru, "Religious Constraints on Reporting HIV/AIDS in Nigeria" http://www.waccglobal.org/en/20072-mediating-the-middle-east/450-Religious-constraints-on-reporting-HIV-AIDS-in-Nigeria.html
6. Irene Ogbogu and Omokhudu Idogho, "The Role of Civil Society Organizations in HIV/AIDS Control," in *AIDS in Nigeria: A Nation on the Threshold,*" eds. Olusoji Adeyi et al., Harvard University Press, 2006, p. 299.
7. 2 Samuel 24, 2. 9–17.
8. Cf. "Essay. An Awakening to AIDS," in *AIDS in Nigeria: A Nation on the Threshold,*" eds. Olusoji Adeyi et al., Harvard University Press, 2006, 4–5. Between 1991 and 2001, Nigeria's prevalence rate grew from 1.8% to 5.8% (UNAIDS Report).
9. These publications include: the 2003 National HIV Sero-Prevalence Sentinel Survey (April 2004); National Workplace Policy on HIV/AIDS (April 2005); National HIV/Syphilis Sero-Prevalence: Sentinel Survey Among Pregnant Women Attending Antenatal Clinics in Nigeria (2005); HIV/STI Integrated Biological and Behavioral Surveillance Survey (2007); HIV Counseling and Testing: Trainee's Manual (2006); The National HIV/AIDS Behavior Change Communication Strategy 2009–2014 (2008).
10. Cf. Jude C. Aguwa: HIV/AIDS in Nigeria, study carried out in 2009 with the Olson Award Grant, Mercy College, NY.
11. *Vanguard* (Nigerian newspaper), Nov. 16, 2008.
12. *Daily Sun* (Nigerian newspaper), April 21, 2009.
13. *Independent* (Nigerian newspaper), Sep. 2, 2008.

14. *Daily Sun*. September 13, 2008. Witchcraft is very common in the traditional religion. While Christianity may condemn indigenous religion as superstitious, the practice of faith healing in Christianity shows that there are some coincidences in their worldviews. This means that the impacts from both indigenous religion and Christianity can converge to build support for supernatural therapeutic system that some naively see as effective even with regard to HIV/AIDS.

15. Claire Mack; Religion and HIV/AIDS in Nigeria" Institute of Global Engagement (December 22, 2006) http://www.globalengage.org/issues/articles/peacemaking/490-religion-and-hiv-aids-in-nigeria.html.

16. Joseph S Gbenda, "Culture-assisted reproduction in Nigeria: the example of the Tiv and Igbo societies" (unpublished paper). The author enumerated various practices in these two communities, which do not allow for limiting sexual activities to the spouses.

17. Catechism of the Catholic Church, #1606.

18. Catholic Secretariat of Nigeria: Nigerian Catholic HIV-AIDS Policy, 2002, page 6.

19. Catechism of the catholic Church, #2370.

20. "The Pope on Condoms and AIDS," *New York Times*, March 19, 2009.

21. Armand Razafimahefa, former head of the Madagascar's Protestant Church, was quoted as saying, "I am firmly opposed to the use of the condom as a means of fighting AIDS, because it promotes promiscuity." http://en.wikipedia.org/wiki/Religion_and_AIDS.

22. "More Respect, not more condoms: A response to Cardinal Pell Response to Media criticism of Pope," by Archbishop John Onaiyekan, Archbishop of Abuja. http://www.Zenit.org/article-25714?=English

23. Kingsley Moghalu: "Fighting AIDS: Africa's Condom Conundrum." http://allafrica.com/stories/200512010200.html.

24. Ibid.

25. "Catholic Church to Ease Ban on Condom Use." http://www.dw-world.de/dw/article/0,2144,1979145,00.html

26. Kingsley Moghalu: "Fighting AIDS: Africa's Condom Conundrum." http://allafrica.com/stories/200512010200.html.

27. Cf. Adedimeji, A., "Perceptions of HIV/AIDS Infection and Condom Use Among Undergraduates in a Nigerian University," in *Nigeria's Contributions to Regional and Global Meetings on HIV/AIDS/STIs 1986–2003*. According to this report: "... almost all those interviewed acknowledged the efficacy of the condom as a barrier method for infection..."

28. Irene Ogbogu and Omokhudu Odogho, "The Role of Civil Society Organizations in HIV/AIDS Control," in *AIDS in Nigeria: A Nation on the Threshold*" eds. Olusoji Adeyi et al., Harvard University Press, 2006, p. 301.

29. Efficacy of a Theory-Based Abstinence-Only Intervention Over Twenty-Four Months, a study reported in *Pediatrics & Adolescent Medicine* (Vol. 164, No. 2, Feb. 2010).

ECOLOGY AND TRADITIONAL CHINESE MEDICINE IN CALIFORNIA

Emily Wu

In traditional Chinese cosmology, which includes contributions from Confucianism, Daoism, Buddhism, and other folk beliefs, the world consists of the heaven above, the earth below, and humans in the middle. The universe and all beings share the basic essence, and all are governed by the same set of principles that not only transcend but also correspond across categories and dimensions. Aspects of the natural world and different dimensions of human existence are categorized according to the shared principles of *yinyang* and five phases,[1] and juxtaposed. Across dimensions and existences those that fall under the same categories share a common set of characteristics and would resonate. In other words, human beings are connected to nature because they correspond with the patterns of heaven and earth, and resonate with the cycles and movements in the environment.

Aside from corresponding patterns, it is also believed that all in the cosmos are composed of and function by the shared life force called *qi*. Health, whether it is human health or environmental health (in Chinese terms, good *fengshui*[2]), is qualified by unobstructed and balanced flow of *qi*.

Traditional Chinese medicine (TCM), a medical system developed with such cosmology as its backdrop, understands the human body and the nature as not only interconnected but also synchronized.[3] In California, where ecological discussions on nature preservation and sustainable living are often informed by multicultural sensitivities and pluralistic spiritual understandings, practitioners of TCM find themselves inevitably contributing to the popular discourse as healers who mediate between Chinese and American cultural systems. Based on ethnographic research in the San Francisco Bay Area[4] (hereafter referred to as the Bay Area), this essay will explore how these practitioners participate in the ecological discourse through their clinical practices and teaching, thereby contributing to the contemporary spiritual discourse in California. (Practitioners in this essay are identified by pseudonyms.)

Practitioners of traditional Chinese medicine in the Bay area

In the past few decades, TCM has become one of the leading alternative medical systems in the United States. In the year of 2001 alone, 2.1 million adults in the United States used acupuncture treatments.[5] California was one of the first states to regulate TCM practitioners, who were, and still are, licensed as acupuncturists. In 1972, the state of California started regulating the practice of acupuncture under the supervision of biomedical physicians; by 1978, acupuncturists in California were already established as primary care providers (who require neither supervision nor referral by biomedical physicians).[6] Approximately half of all licensed acupuncturists in the United States currently practice in California.[7] By May 2009, a total of 13,110 acupuncture licenses had been issued in California, more than doubled the count of 6,300 licenses in 2000.[8] Approximately one-fifth of all licensed acupuncturists in California are currently practicing in the San Francisco Bay Area. According to a survey I conducted in 2006 on TCM practitioners across California, the profession consisted of 41% Caucasian American, 44% Chinese American, 10% other Asian Americans, and a small percentage of mixed and other ethnics; as I conducted fieldwork in the Bay Area, I found the ethnic demographic of TCM practitioners similarly composed.[9]

Legally regulated by the state, and where more than half of the licensed practitioners are non-Chinese ethnics and largely American (Caucasian American), TCM provides services largely in the American mainstream. In the context of United States, within the predominantly biomedical framework, TCM is a complementary and alternative medicine (CAM) that originated from China. Contrasted with biomedicine as the "conventional" medicine,[10] the CAMs are positioned on the periphery and are marginal to the standards and values of Western biomedicine. Furthermore, the "traditional" and "indigenous" labels also contrast against the assumed "modernism" of biomedicine. Not only does TCM become indigenized in the American context, the profession has also reconfigured itself to also serve functions that venture into the realms of psychological, religious,[11] and spiritual.[12] Categorized under the umbrella of CAM, practitioners of TCM in America, especially but not exclusively those who are not Chinese ethnics, often incorporate the central beliefs and values of the general CAM into their practices and ideology—Holism, Vitalism, spiritual usage of secular language, understanding of health as a state of optimal conditions rather than only the absence of symptoms, and the teamwork relationship between healer and patient.[13]

In turn, key concepts in TCM, such as *jing qi shen* 精氣神 (essence, *qi*, and spirit), the relationships and interactions between *yin* and *yang* and between the five elements, are interpreted through the lenses of the above-mentioned CAM ideologies.

The ecological discourse in the TCM clinics emerges from this cross-cultural attempt to demonstrate the understanding of human existence as an in integral, synchronized part of the great cosmos.

Attention to transformative effects of the immediate environment
From clinic visits, I found that there is a wide range of individual styles among the TCM clinics—some are sterile and functional, some are quiet and minimalist, some are warm and filled with the scent of herbs, some aim to relax with dim light and soft music, still others reflect the particular aesthetic preferences of the practitioners in charge. Despite the varying presentations, there is a shared attention to the clinic ambience. My 2006 survey found that practitioners not only want the first impressions on their clinics to be professional, but many also aim to evoke the feelings of comfort, calm, relaxation, safety, and peacefulness.[14] At the TCM school's community clinics, where new practitioners were trained, the group treatment sessions also provided patients with hot mint tea (which filled the room with a comforting fragrance), indirect and dimmed lighting, soft background music, and whispering practitioners.

Perhaps spa-like in appearance, TCM practitioners often emphasize the importance of the transformative power of appropriate clinic ambience. Allison, a Caucasian American practitioner and TCM theories instructor at the local TCM school, articulates:

> It's not something I can put into words, but I can say, it's the flow and movement in the space. The other people in the space. There is something about what energy is left there by people or brought there by people. The colors. The amount of light. Plants. All of those things. They are all small things in a way, but as a whole... I've had people who, I can remember recently someone came in the wrong time for their appointment. ...She said, just sitting in your waiting room, I sat and I felt so peaceful in there that I just felt better when I left. Even though, you know, she just sat in there. That is really important to me.[15]

In short, the healing process can start from the moment a patient steps into the clinic. It may be without a direct treatment session with the practitioner; on the other hand, the clinic ambience as the creation of a practitioner resonates with the intention of the practitioner.

If ambience is indirect presence or extension of the presence of the practitioner, practitioners also cultivate themselves to amplify their healing efficacy in the clinic. By cultivation, I include practices that are commonly known as "cultivation practices," where the shared goal of the activities is to cultivate the person, whether it is physically, emotionally, psychologically, or spiritually. When I approached practitioners with the concepts, they listed exercises they do to make connections between the physical and the spiritual, between outer and the inner, between the individual and the nature, etc. Some listed sports regimens and explained that the physical exercises help them get "more in tune with their own bodies." Secular sports can possibly serve the same purpose as many of the more physically oriented cultivation practices.[16] Although many expressed that they do not necessarily tell patients about their personal cultivation practices, when asked how relevant these practices are to their clinical practices, only 10% who responded think they are not relevant. Seventy-two percent of the respondents think that these practices are either very helpful or extremely important to their clinical practices.[17]

Estelle, a young Caucasian American practitioner who is building her patient base by working in two clinics, shares how her personal cultivation helps with her clinical treatments:

> I realized if I do have a daily spiritual practice I would feel a lot better—more centered and calm. So I can't honestly say that I follow one religion; I definitely don't go to church or anything like that. I'm not a big believer of that. But I do have my daily meditative spiritual practice, and I do yoga a lot. To me that's like my spiritual practice, because before and after [treatment sessions] I meditate for like 10 minutes. To me that's when I feel the most...
> I guess when what people feel like when their doing their religious practice, which is light and solitary.
> I need to feel centered to be able to be there for my patients fully. I know the days I'm off: maybe it doesn't come across to the patients, because my nature is...people think I am very together and grounded. But if you're having a bad day, it is so hard to be present.[18]

Rafael, a Chinese-speaking Caucasian American practitioner who teaches Medical Chinese in the local TCM school, establishes the connection from the perspective of oneness:

> [My mentor] said to me, "So one thing that you need to start to think about and cultivate is this very very clear realization that when a patients comes into the clinic, and they're sitting there in front of you, that it's just one of YOU in the room."
> And I know that just yesterday when I was seeing patients I thought about that at one point, I thought about it at a few different points with two different patients, and I remembered that the awareness came in, and it felt like the whole treatment just went smoothly from that perspective. It's a beautiful way to approach life, right, but in that particular context the medical context.
> I guess it is sort of like meditation in a way you just visualize it, or you have that intention. I don't know how much of it comes from my previous exposure doing spiritual practices, but it's just a question of constant practice and cultivating our mind and

refining our vision, and the way we experience ourselves in the world. It's just kind of a split second of remembering, and it's totally mysterious, and I don't understand it. It's just this cool concept, but I feel like there is something to it, like when I do remember that, I feel like the whole treatments just unfolds in this much more natural, don't know if it is spontaneous. Yeah, it just feels like it goes better.[19]

Several other practitioners also say that self-cultivation helps them perform more effective treatments and stay energized for the long workdays. By connecting to nature and tapping into the universal *qi*, practitioners become grounded, centered, and energetically resourceful for the needs of their patients. By connecting to the patients, the practitioners become channels through which the patients benefit from not only the treatment but also from the healing effect of the environment.

Illness causation explanations

When I queried the TCM practitioners about their perspective on the causes of disease (and symptoms, for those who separate disease etiology from symptoms), two trends emerged from the collected data: (1) Most practitioners believe that there are multiple causes of disease in the human body; and (2) Instead of the classically TCM etiology, the most popularly identified causes of disease are actually a mixture of biomedical and holistic categories. Unhealthy Lifestyle is the most emphasized cause of disease (88%), followed by Disharmony between Body and Mind (79%). These two chart toppers are main concerns in holistic medicine, where proper lifestyle and the harmonious integration of dimensions such as mind, body, and spirit are believed to lead to overall health of a person. The next two most popular causes are biomedical categories: Pathogens (65%) and Pollutant and Chemicals (60%). Even Blockage, a keyword in the energy paradigm, only gets identified by 48% of the respondents. The classical TCM etiological categories such as Excess/Deficiency (33%) and Wind (32%) are not as highly recognized as the prior terms.[20]

In other words, TCM practitioners in California focus on how their patients carry themselves and relate to the environment (Unhealthy Lifestyle and Disharmony between Body and Mind) more than using the classical TCM disease explanations of internal imbalance (Excess/Deficiency) and external invasions (Wind) or the biomedical diagnosis of infections (Pathogens) and poisoning (Pollutants and Chemicals). Although it is recognized that some patients are ill due to reasons that they have no control over, a commonly held position among practitioners is that the patients can achieve better health if they assume responsibility to achieve it through cultivating better habits and connection between the physical and beyond-physical, between the self and nature.

When patients seem open to the idea of self-cultivation, sometimes practitioners would recommend that their patients pick up a practice too. Among those practitioners I talked to, many share their cultivation methods with their patients, mostly informally. A few teach more formally: one practitioner teaches yoga classes in the studio behind her clinic, another teaches free *qigong* classes in the local park on the weekends, yet another, a Chinese immigrant practitioner, opens his home kitchen to patients and teach them raw food preparations. Here we see the transfer of responsibility of healing from the practitioner to the patients. The responsibility, whether it is in the form of practicing to cultivate and strengthen one's *qi* and connection with the universal *qi* or to prepare health-enhancing food, is to make positive changes in one's lifestyle.

Juxtaposing human and nature

In a public lecture in 2008, sinologist and historian of Chinese medicine Paul Unschuld shared a cross-cultural shift he observes in the TCM theoretical paradigm in the United States: Historically a mainly agrarian culture, Chinese traditionally analogizes human bodily functions with water irrigations and rivers; on the other hand, non-Chinese American TCM practitioners and patients, first introduced to TCM during an era of energy crisis, understand human mechanisms through the analogy of energy, where human body is seen as something like a battery.[21] In the Bay Area where China-trained practitioners and educators are numerous and active, I observe a coexistence and sometimes a mixture of both paradigms.

George, a Chinese ethnic practitioner who teaches Chinese medical classics in the local TCM school, explains human physiological mechanism by corresponding with natural phenomena. Here he talks about the cause and treatment strategy for diabetes:

In Chinese medicine, meridians are rivers. In the human body there are four seas, the brain, bones, blood, and *qi*; four seas. The four seas are connected by the blood vessels in the body, and the meridians are rivers. In these rivers, cholesterol corresponds with the Earth phase. Sugar is sweet, among the five phases, the taste that corresponds with earth is sweetness. Metal corresponds with spiciness, Fire corresponds with bitterness, Wood corresponds with sourness, and water corresponds with saltiness. Fatty things and muscles are related to the spleen, and spleen corresponds with Earth. When more of these [Earthy] things accumulate inside the blood vessels, like eating too greasy, these accumulate, it's like a lot of soil in water, like the Yellow River [in China]. Yellow River is in a condition of high cholesterol. Why high cholesterol? The river bed gets higher and higher. How high? It's now more than twenty meters higher than the cities by the river. Once the levees breaks, think about it, the cities must be flooded. But how did the river bed get so high? Because the river bed has a lot of soil…soil is earth, and it is just like the lipid and blood sugar inside blood vessels. How does TCM treat that? Western medicine treats high blood pressure by reducing the pressure: when there is a lot of blood, it exerts more pressure on the blood vessels, so they use diuretics. Why use diuretics? Because they want to reduce the volume of the blood. Just like nowadays, the Yellow River is treated, they drain out the water in it by branching it out.

That is one way, but not the best way, and not a way to treat the root of the problem, just treating the symptoms. So what is the way to treat the root problem? At least we need to take away some of that soil, that is the train of thought toward treating the root problem, removing the Earth. How do you remove the Earth? You can't just dig, but there is more soil continuously coming down from upstream, and after you dig some, more soil comes along. The source of the problem is whether there are trees upstream. If there are trees and they are all green, the tree roots stabilize the soil [by holding on to soil] and there won't be lost soil [going down stream]. Trees are woods, and liver corresponds with Wood [element], so the root problem of diabetes is in the liver. If the liver is taken care of, [the person] is happy, with nothing to stress over and nothing to worry about, then there is no diabetes or high blood pressure. It works great.[22]

George's explanation is clearly the irrigation analogy that Unschuld insightfully identifies in traditional Chinese medical paradigm.

I have heard the energy analogy as well. A Caucasian American clinical training instructor in the TCM school explains how she determines her treatment plan depending on the time of the day:

> If the patients come in earlier in the day, then I would sometimes put a needle in to boost the energy, that way they will be energized for the rest of the day. But if the patients come at the end of the day, then I would do a calming needle so that they can go home, relax, and have a good night sleep.[23]

This is indeed analogizing the human body as a battery, where one would want to charge it up for an active day, or drain it down for a restful night. Using needles, *qigong*, and other cultivation and healing methods, humans are connected to the universe much like small electronics connect to chargers.

Ecological awareness and responsibility

Mostly through practice and action, many TCM practitioners connect themselves to nature, their environment, and their patients to reinforce their healing. Beyond training their patients into becoming more aware of what they *take in* from nature—for examples, ingesting only healthy food and dietary supplements suitable to one's specific constitution, and avoiding herbs polluted by pesticides and harmful minerals—some practitioners also discuss with their patients about what goes back into nature. Besides topics on recycling, energy conservation, and lower car emissions, the most unique type of "pollution" talked about in the TCM clinics is *qi* pollution. The logic goes as follow: since we all share the universal *qi* and are connected by it, then the diseased or negative *qi* (*bingqi* 病氣) can also be contagious even if the illness itself is not pathologically infectious. Therefore, if that particular *qi* is not properly neutralized, it can become unwanted pollution to make more people and the environment sick.

Practitioners who cultivate regularly strengthen themselves to protect against such *qi* pollution. In fact, some Chinese ethnic practitioners have explained to me that the reason why physical cultivation is especially important for a healer is that one must strengthen his or her own protective *qi* to stay healthy while spending so much time in the clinic with patients. A few Caucasian practitioners who have backgrounds in visualization meditations say that they visualize a transparent barrier between them and the patients.

Sally, who is the director of the medical *qigong* program in a TCM school, uses *qigong* healing regularly in her private clinical practice. I asked her if she does anything to protect herself from diseased *qi*, or if she has strategies to cleanse or neutralize a space that has been occupied by a patient who may have very potent *qi*. Sally describes her procedure for keeping the treatment rooms and her clinic free of potentially injurious *qi*:

> When I treat a patient, I also create a vortex in the room that sucks the bad *qi* out of the room. It's like a tornado that directs diseased *qi* away and keeps the room clean and ready for the next patient.[24]

Sally is not explicit about how such a vortex is created, but the concept sounds a lot like a kitchen vent that expels smoke and odor out of the house. The implication of such procedure to become part of her clinical routine is that it is likely that it is also part of the standardized treatment procedure in medical *qigong* practices in the Bay Area, or at least for students who attend the certificate program that she directs.

Ashley, another practitioner who incorporates *qigong* healing into her acupuncture practice, uses large pieces of jade and blessed blankets from her *qigong* master to neutralize diseased *qi*. When I observed at her clinic, she showed me pieces of jade with black spots—signs of diseased *qi* being absorbed by the jade. She said it takes a while for the jade pieces to neutralize themselves, whereupon the black spots would disappear. I mentioned to her a common practice to neutralize stones and crystals energetically: by placing it under running water. Ashley disapproves of the practice: "The water will take away the diseased *qi*, but then it goes down the drain and goes into the rivers and the ocean. We shouldn't be polluting nature that way."[25]

Instead, Ashley prefers to rotate the jade pieces for them to neutralize naturally, and to chant upon the bless blankets to help them clear from the diseased *qi* they absorb during treatments.

Some practitioners also promote healthy lifestyle and environmental awareness by providing reading materials in only those genres in their clinics. For example, Ashley only has yoga, vegetarian diet, and healthy lifestyle magazines in the waiting area; on her receptionist counter are information on nutritional supplements and occasional fliers for lost pets in the local community. Another practitioner stated bluntly: "I don't want trashy magazines polluting my patients while they wait for me to fix them."[26]

TCM, spirituality, and ecological discourse

Traditional Chinese medicine, as a medical system that theorizes based on the assumption of transcendent nature of *qi*, provides the space for spiritual dialogs in the clinical setting by recognizing an inherent connection between human and nature. With the TCM practitioners, from the physical sensation of *qi* movements and the experiences of enhanced healing effects after their self-cultivation, there is often a deeply felt connection with and appreciation for the environment.[27] From the perspective of many of these TCM practitioners, the environment must be protected not only because humans are part of it, but because humans inevitably resonates with every aspect of it by sharing the same essential substance, or breath—the *qi*. As healers participating in the Californian ecological discourse, the practitioners not only focus on restoring and maintaining the health of their patients, but also engage themselves in actively improving and preserving the environment that contributes to the general well-being of all existences within it. As I have demonstrated in this essay, the efforts manifest in several dimensions of TCM clinical practices: from the attention to details in creating a transformative clinical environment to cultivating themselves to provide more effective healing, to educating the patients into assuming responsibility in maintaining healthy lifestyles, to promoting ecological awareness and actions to preserve and protect the environment.

Currently, TCM in California is not yet making significant impact on the global production of TCM knowledge that mostly takes place in the People's Republic of China. However, as TCM in America continues to mature and evolve, we might see the ecological sensitivity that was developed in California become recognized on a more global scale.

Notes

1. *Yinyang* and the Five Phases (Metal, Wood, Water, Fire, and Earth) are fundamental theories in Chinese philosophy that go back as far as the Han dynasty (206 B.C.E.–220 C.E.). They are used to first describe patterns and cycles observed in nature, but the resulting rules extend to all realms of human existence—the functions of the human body, interactions between people, landscaping and geomancy, politics, etc. For a brief explanation of *yinyang* and Five Phases theories, see Livia Kohn, *Daoism and Chinese Culture* (Cambridge, MA: Three Pine Press, 2001), 44–47; for medical application of the Five Phases theory, see Ted. J. Kaptchuk, *The Web That Has No Weaver: Understanding Chinese Medicine* (New York: McGraw-Hill, 2000), 437–452.
2. *Fengshui*, literally meaning wind and water in Chinese, is an art to find the most optimal location, orientation, and composition of a space for the people residing in or using it. When the *fengshui* of a space is ideal, energy within flows smoothly, and people feel comfortable in it and will prosper in all aspects in life.
3. My usage of the term TCM includes a wide variety of practices under the broader umbrella of Chinese medicine, rather than as the equivalent of state-regulated TCM in the People's Republic of China (PRC-TCM).
4. The Bay Area consists of counties that share the Oakland-San Francisco-San Jose metropolitan core. In this study, I include ten counties that surround the inner San Francisco Bay: Alameda, Contra Costa, Marin, Napa, San Francisco, San Mateo, Santa Clara, Santa Cruz, Solano, and Sonoma.
5. See National Center for Complementary and Alternative Medicines (NCCAM, part of the National Institute of Health) website: http://nccam.nih.gov/health/acupuncture/#ususe
6. See State of California Department of Consumer Affairs Acupuncture Board website: http://www.acupuncture.ca.gov/about_us/history.shtml.
7. See Hans A. Baer, *Toward an Integrative Medicine: Merging Alternative Therapies with Biomedicine* (Walnut Creek, CA: AltaMira Press, 2004), 49.
8. The licensee count for 2000 can be found in University of California, San Francisco commissioned vocational report on Acupuncture, 2004. I arrived at the May 2009 license count by going directly to the license verification engine, accessible for the general public, on the State of California Acupuncture Board website, http://www2.dca.ca.gov/pls/wllpub/wllqryna$lcev2.startup?p_qte_code=AC&p_qte_pgm_code=6500. More about statistical information of licensed acupuncturists in the Bay Area can be found in the next chapter.
9. Five hundred surveys were mailed to TCM practitioners across California, where 138 practitioners responded. During my intensive fieldwork in the San Francisco Bay Area from 2008 to 2009, I conducted formal interviews with forty-five practitioners. I also visited

twenty-five of the practitioners' private clinics and two clinics run by the local TCM schools. All the names of my informants here are pseudonyms.

10. NCCAM, part of NIH, defines complementary and alternative medicine as "as group of diverse medical and health care systems, practices, and products that are not presently considered to be part of conventional medicine." See http"//nccam.nih.gov/news/camsurvey_fs1.htm. Accessed October 7, 2007.

11. Linda L. Barnes, "The Psychologizing of Chinese Healing Practices in the United States," *Culture, Medicine, and Psychiatry* 22 (1998): 413–443.

12. This is to indicate that spiritual can be beyond religious, or at least institutionally religious, and to reflect the preference of some practitioners who identify as "spiritual but not religious."

13. See Michael S. Goldstein, "The Emerging Socioeconomic and Political Support for Alternative Medicine in the United States," *Annals of the American Academy of Political and Social Science: Global Perspectives on Complementary and Alternative Medicine* 583 (2002): 44–63; Bonnie B. O'Connor, *Healing Traditions: Alternative Medicine and the Health Professions* (Philadelphia: University of Pennsylvania Press, 1995); Peter A. Clark, "The Ethics of Alternative Medicine," *Journal of Public Health Policy* 21, no. 4 (2000): 447–470; J. A. English-Lueck, *Health in the New Age: A Study in California Holistic Practices* (Albuquerque: University of New Mexico Press, 1990). Holism here is defined as the belief that the whole is greater than the sum of its parts, with emphasis on individual differences and complexity of factors causing illness, and a deliberate break from mind–body dualism. Vitalism consists of beliefs that there is a life force that suffuses the human body, which is health and healing promoting when it is sufficient and balanced, and illness inducing if blocked or unbalanced.

14. The open-ended survey question was What first impression do the practitioners want the patients to have upon arriving at their clinics? Respondents listed their own adjectives. Fifty percent of the respondents listed professional as the impression they want their patients to have upon entering their clinic. But that was only the second highest ranking. Adjectives that suggest the atmosphere of a Sanctuary (safe, healing, calming, relaxing, soothing, etc.) ranked the highest at 58%. Related to Sanctuary are adjectives that suggest peacefulness (peaceful, still, and quiet) which were also listed by 30% of the respondents.

15. Personal Communication, November 12, 2008.

16. In my survey, only 15 out of 138 respondents either did not do any of these practices or chose not to answer. The rest of the respondents checked from one to many of the items on the list as activities they regularly practice. More than half (53%) of the respondents say that they try to get in touch with nature regularly; it is interesting to note that this is popular even with people who do not have other "practices." Sitting Meditation is the next popular activity (37%), with *qigong* exercises (31%) and Taichi. Exercises (28%) to follow. Praying to god, Allah, or the goddess is regularly practiced by 25% of the respondents, while communicating with spiritual beings and forces is also favored by 25% of the respondents. There is a clear trend of regularly practicing to become more in tune with the environment, the cosmos, and within oneself; in other words, we can safely say that the TCM practitioners are doing a fair amount of spiritual cultivation in their private time.

17. Percentages come from my 2006 survey.

18. Personal Communication, September 3, 2008.

19. Personal Communication, November 7, 2008.
20. The numeric data are collected through my 2006 survey. A similar trend was observed in my formal interviews.
21. Paul Unschuld, "Chinese Medicine and Western Healthcare Systems: Is Integration Possible?" (Public lecture in Berkeley, CA, November 11, 2008).
22. Personal Communication, October 18, 2008.
23. Personal Communication, September 23, 2008.
24. Personal Communication, January 29, 2009.
25. Personal Communication, October 2, 2009.
26. Personal Communication, April 19, 2008.
27. Without using the terminology, many practitioners in the Bay Area promote what scholars of ecological discourses call "deep ecology," which is a "deeply felt spiritual connections to the earth's living systems and ethical obligations to protect them." See Bron Taylor and Michael Zimmerman, "Deep Ecology" in *Encyclopedia of Religion and Nature* (London: Continuum, 2005), 456–459.

HIP-HOP PERCUSSION AND CUBIST VISION
"Africa" Climbing the Spine Like an Unwanted Mime at the Post-colonial Crossroads

Jim Perkinson

This essay begins somewhere downside of the word up.
The *New York Times* of October 30, 2005, reports on a new Alzheimer's treatment it calls "The Pablo Picasso Therapy." Sitting in front of the Malagueño painter's 1932 picture titled "Girl Before a Mirror," an 88-year-old former real estate broker—dyspeptic, cantankerous, fixated in confusion at the edge of a chasm, at the precipice of the void he stares into every day as the march of memory loss advances—says suddenly, astonishingly, "It's like he's trying to tell a story using words that don't exist. He knows what he means, but we don't" (Kennedy, 1D). Here, at the crossroads between narrative representation and expressive conjuration, where story stands mute before its genesis in inchoate groan and wordless bone patterns, something is happening outside the Western text of healing. Speech is being animated by color. Memory is finding restoration in fractured gesture. An old body is suddenly moved like a young volcano. The dementia-word waxes melodic from a scrambled lip code, freed by the base beat of a visual throb of paint, itself a haint of power channeled through the Andalusian-Jew-Spaniard's palette by a portent pirated from Africa's Dahomey more than 100 years ago, as we shall see below (Salmon, 81–82).

In Detroit in 1999, at a conference at the Institute of the Arts, after a presentation of the history of hip-hop up to that moment by a post-modern African-American poet/activist, a white kid in his early twenties, baggy pants, cap on backwards, gesturing "typically," stands up and says earnestly, unapologetically, naively, "Hip-hop—I would die for this shit!"

That "shit," of course, had begun before his birth, in the South Bronx in the 1970s, when an impossible adolescence, arched in agony above broken brick and ripped pipe, weed-wild-lot and garbage-gutted-gutter, had spun on head to heavy dub and hard drone of a DJ Kool Herc amp-mix, ricocheting like syncopated trance of high romance bubble, between eight-story apartment building sides in a sonic ride of inner-city bromide against the tide of early death. In a later coming into this insane game of break-neck b-boy-and-girl meeting Flash-fingered-sample warped in a Wizard-wipe-scratch of vinyl, giving aural texture and somatic-signature to the outlaw tag of turf, rap emerged like a slow-growing tsunami of the tongue. Here, the word had begun ancillary, secondary, served as mere filler over the real-deal thump under the rib—occupying minds with entertainment signs, while the DJ-ed feet negotiated the harsh heat of a concrete street-mortality—before that word found its own stature in the 80s as a freestyling capture of ring-shout cipher-rapture, wrapping an entire globe in a high-tech-probe of low-down-truth.

In one case, a splash of color, provoking an old mind back to life; in the other, a sonic flash stirring a young body to (im)possible sacrifice! Between these two worlds—the visual rub of a polymorphic plasticity giving rise to the word and the sonic drub of a polyrhythmic sagacity preceding the word—the entire Western world is queried like a quarry of rock and demons (Read, 96, 144).

The essay to follow will focus on this unanticipated convergence of "African" traditions of percussive insurgence rupturing modernist consciousness from within, beginning as early as Picasso's appropriation of "instinctual things" in mask-forms adopted from the mother-continent and as late as rap riffs giving rise to rhythmic trips around the planet in the new millennium. Auguring like a sign of the times at the edge of both aesthetic traditions is the "potency of heightened contrast" derived from what Robert Farris Thompson would call the syncopated stylistics of African poetics and hip-hop scholar Tricia Rose shouts out as "ruptured flow." "Africa" here is not offered as essence, but rather as place-marker for the continent furthest out in transnational capitalism's 500- year-old project of pirating and stockpiling global resources (for its white-faced sorcerers) and simultaneously race-marker for the skin-tone forced deepest down in the social hierarchies resulting from Western reproduction of itself all over the planet. But this same

"Africa" is now also post-modern signal of shared genetic ancestry in biology and paradoxically projected in hip-hoppery as feared/desired destiny. That the 20th century has been torn by an aesthetic break with Euro-traditions of realism in the direction of a clearly African-originated fascination with polyphony in sound and polymorphism in vision is comprehended not as mere fashion, but a deeper symptom of history. That symptom will be offered as exposé of the strangeness of color-oppression historically and of the "return of the repressed" inside white presumptions of superiority in the contemporary post-colony. In hip-hop today as in cubism yesterday, "Africa" can be observed erupting all over the world as the great anonymous question of the time: whence have we come and wither are we going at this late date of seemingly ill-fate on planet Earth?

Cubist geometry generated by African ontology

There is a recognized conundrum in the aesthetics of modern painting. It is clear Picasso, Braque and crew broke out of their assigned pew in the canons of conventional European representation one hundred years ago. But the Cubism that began to come into view in 1907 was only the first break with the supposed sacredness of that particular tradition of the canvas. The entire motley posse of Western painterly wildness since then has felt the fall of the spell, smelled primal energies inside indigenous synergies, rifled the resident plunder of colonial sunderings of artifacts from natives, smoked novelty like a toke, spoken in tongues through their fingers, while their heads thundered without a lightning strike to illumine the landscape of their new desires. The significance erupted like an epiphany of blood, singing without signs, rupturing every design of syntax and palette. The target was the hegemony of light, plundered by photography, painted by Impression, revealing the fiction of things in the eye. Stranger by far, suddenly, were things not as they appeared in mediation by vision, but in the deep set "why" of existence, the "sigh" of things as they conjured human passion, under the skin (i.e., modern art as an exploration of the dictum that "exactitude is not truth," says writer Herbert Read; Read, 44). Cezanne had begun the break down, Matisse and his Fauvist zoo of French "beasts" continued the surcease of convention, Cubist angularity divined the geometry of the epiphany, Germanic Expressionist confession—whether Dresden's

Die Brucke version or Munich's *Blaue Reiter* stew—augured deep into the steep depths of human mystery and rue-ing of destiny by means of distortion and color, Futurism manifesto-ed the mad vortex of dynamic materiality driving modernity like a sudden soliloquy of divinity, Dadaist destruction, Surrealist automatism, the abstract constructivism of a Kandinsky or Klee, or the provocative sensationalism of Pollock, plying his paste like an Navajo sand painter wanna-be—all cut loose from the old dock and plied waters dark and brewing (Read, 34, 54, 65–66, 70, 110, 120, 194, 220–222, 267). But again and again in this "news" of modernity's break with the painterly past, we find side reference to indigeneity, especially in its African or "negro" views (Read, 62). And begging attention at the heart of the mix is the first fix on this prolixity of nature and creativity: the African mask appearing as Picasso face on two of the figures of his 1907 *Les Demoiselles d'Avignon* (Read, 68).

Picasso is renowned as roving eclectic—ventriloquizing Catalonian Romanesque alongside the Spanish El Greco grotesque, Gothic spectral fantasy shimmering over Fauvian tumult—but Cezanne remained regular touchstone and, in the case of the *d'Avignon* piece, narrative outline inside of which Picasso iconically tattooed something else (Read, 68, 18). That "something else" has provoked speculative congress ever since. Already, according to a Carl Jung commentary (on the 1932 "Girl in the Mirror" canvas), Picasso in his Blue Period before 1907 had been exploring interminably, if unconsciously, what Jung calls the *Nekyia,* the journey to Hades, leaving behind the day-world of light for the "blue of night, of moonlight and water, the *Tuat*-blue of the Egyptian underworld" in a soul-journey from which he perhaps never quite fully returned (Jung, 137–138). (Patently—an underworld with real over-world reference among the proletariat—a blues of down-and-out, working peoples' poverty and despair, that would provoke its own Rose Period rejoinder in Picasso's palette and psyche.) Of course Jung's associations here reproduce Western imaginings of African doings in stereotypic form—but even stereotypes can harbor truth in upside-down tropes, as we shall see. By 1906, however, on regular visits to Matisse's house for dinner, Picasso began to encounter the "Negro sculpture" that poet-friend Max Jacob opines is the birth mother of Cubism (Jacob, 202).

Within short order, says Jacob, Picasso "absorbed himself in deep meditation, simplifying animals and objects and arriving at a single stroke at drawings of a kind that recall those in prehistoric caves" (Jacob, 202). The association with shamanic decomposition is prescient (as covered below). Writer-raconteur Andre Salmon will say of the same moment of ferment that in his ardor, already the artist had placed "the sculpture of the Negroes above the Egyptians" and had begun himself to emerge as a modern "apprentice sorcerer seeking answers among the enchantments of Oceania and Africa" (Salmon, 81–82). *Demoiselles* became the playground of the encounter, hosting spirits of experiment like a cinematic séance, without a guide at the table to interpret the possession. Strikingly, this canvas was never presented by Picasso to the public, but "regularly turned to the wall" after the artist had once again re-invented his world on its ever-changing surface. The masks that popped out on the top of the nude right-hand bodies figured a desperate clash of titans, sharp-edged images articulating rugged desires, postmarking the collision of cultures, the great metabolism of Africa and elsewhere by European colonial rapacity. As Salmon would say, the result was a "philosophical brothel," a "picture-as-equation," masks pushing away from the merely human, beyond allegory, neither gods nor heroes, but "naked problems, white numbers on the blackboard" (Salmon, 81–82). Perhaps today, we might more accurately re-play the tryst in reverse—blackface mime climbing the spine of a white-minded design, like a sign of the still-living dead, mounting the head, unread and unreadable, by Picasso and his culture. Those faces still augur the times in a strange rhyme of the climb of Africa onto the white surface of global capital. But I get ahead of the line here.

Henry Read summarizes the Cubist breakthrough of this new "something" inside the old Cezannean structure as a "geometricization of the sharply outlined figures," a direct transposition of "the rationality of African negro sculpture into pictorial compositions," abandoning Cezanne's principle of modulation in favor of a fragmentation of form, an angular distortion of the subject similar to a mirror-glass mosaic of reflections (Read, 70, 75, 78). As a moment of "liberation" transforming the art of the "whole world" (sic) in the aftermath of the First World War, for Read, this organically creative energy represents a drive toward a basic grammar of the object, a kind of shamanic dismemberment of the surface of things, we might rejoin, seeking to agitate human sensibility by proceeding not from perception to representation, but from the former straight to imagination, "breaking down the perceptual images in order to re-combine them in a non-representational (rational or conceptual) structure" (Read, 87, 96–97, 144). The process involved a principled "free association" of subjects, culled, in the case of Picasso and Braque, from the iconography of the Parisian studio and café, to be sure, but driving toward a textured *collage* of the *motif* with much broader ramifications: an architectonics of sensorial intensity, disavowing the unity of the image in favor of its mystery and multiplicity, in which the historical horror of modernity's unconscious can be discerned breaking out in a kinesthetic abstraction of reference bearing global significance for a world under the domination of Euro-realist reason and control (Read, 98, 100–101, 144, 162, 180). Here, we might venture, is colonialism's repressed returning with a vengeance inside the Western canon of beauty.

But in any case, at the heart of such a mouthful of claims, tellingly, is the constant appendage of the term "rhythm" to the painterly vision, a "simultaneity-fusion" rebelling against the bourgeois tyranny of harmony and good taste, that expresses time and space through an "abstract presentation of motion" (Read, 140, 110, 113). "Noise music" is offered by Read as a Dadaist correlate that surfaces in the 1920s in the key of aurality (Read, 117). But it is perhaps not until the aftermath of Black Power reversals of the public signatures of race in America in the 1960s, detonated in sound in the decades following as the assault rhythms of "reality rap" and Public Enemy's *Bring the Noise*, that we meet the deep political significance of this early 20th century visual breakout. Cubism and its successors remained largely *avant-garde*; hip-hop, on the other hand, goes popular and planetary by the end of the millennium, probing the pain of ghettos black and rainbow before their explosions in flame and bullets in South Central Los Angeles in 1992 and north Paris, France, in 2005. Rap and its repertoires are prophetic, grenades of sound and form before the social fact of upheaval. But their aesthetic is clearly Afrocentric, a working of the sharp edges of contradictions demographic and sociopathic, given focus and finesse in the stylistics of a staccato dialectic that is both black Atlantic in origin and Afrodiasporic in concern. The pathology probed in these "percussive epistemologies" is the West *writ large*. Here, the genealogy of Pablo's *Desmoiselles* meets its progeny in a 21st century Outlandish melody "specifyin' Moorishly on" the cacophony of 2Pac's post-industrial *Makaveli*—a globalized ghetto-grin riding hard on top of the digitalized cyber-flesh of late capital, like Picasso-esque masks in post-modern possession of the new techno-body of whiteness.

Hip-hop polyphony as apocalypse of western hegemony

Whatever else it is—and hip-hop culture is at least a multivalent "sign of the times" if not an ironic mime of the entire late capitalist design to relocate the whole world, including everything oppositional to its own sublime collateral, inside a commodity—hip-hop is a mode of signification *on* neo-liberal globalization. Growing out of an early 1970s breakdown of the industrial regime in urban centers losing expertise to the suburbs, and skills to machines, and jobs to the Japanese and other global competitors, the subculture of rap, scratch, uprock, and rollicking tag of turf, embodies a much older tradition of toast, roast, woof, and boast that it both samples and tramples upon. Henry Louis Gates Jr. has noted some 26 rhetorical "tropes" (figures of speech) in the African-American repertoire alone that carry out the intention or effect of referencing and "trumping" previous speakers in the process of updating, displacing, playing with or putting down what has come before (Gates, 78). And in citing Gates Jr., I could just as easily nod to Michael Eric Dyson Sr., Zora Neale Hurston and Toni Morrison, Richard Wright and Ralph Ellison, Richard Pryor and Charlie Parker, and thousands upon thousands of anonymous word-barkers and horn-squallers, drum-rollers, and tale-tellers and proverb-proliferating-provocateurs across 500 years of Western/African contact that have all continuously brought Afro-centrifugal conventions of expressive innovation to bear on, and to hidden efflorescence within, Euro-dominant strategies of control, in the academy and street alike.

Gates merely points out that this constant riff upon one's predecessors—at once honoring and correcting—instantiates what he calls a conscious focus upon the Signifier in communication—a paradigmatic proliferation of the possibilities of meaning-making in the very act of communicating that revels in "swinging" the medium itself in the direction of an infinite piracy and play, rather than reifying the (syntagmatic) presumption of policing and imprisoning meaning inside of a sentence or sound (Gates, 49). This celebration of the Signifier over the Signified embodied historically in Yoruban and Fon invocations of the trickster-haunt of all choices and crossroads (Eshu-Elegbara in Nigeria and Legba in Benin) is the very thing that finally found European fortune and fame in Picasso's primitivist-modern focus on form over content (in the ultimate extent of which form actually became the content) (Warncke, 71). Hip-hop is simply the latest round in this "profligacy of possibility" that of old took shape in the mold of the Signifying Monkey of West African and southern plantation fame, taming the jungle-powers of lion and master alike, white-supremacist elephant-on-the-table-of post-bellum-polity or ex-slave-sycophant-trying-to-suck-the-teat-of-fast-retreating-Republicans-building-a-party-on-a-disingenuous-platform-of-equality. Street signifying, in the state of things in early 20th century America, became a survival game, training young black minds to spit out the rind of insult while preserving the cult of a public "be happy" to avoid a knappy-headed hanging. Hip-hop continues the tradition of a "spitting revision" of oppression—but now post-Civil Rights and Black Power, where the 'hood no longer cowers before the white-sheeted broker of things acceptable. In this latest mobilization of the energies of a dozens-playing virtuosity, the word is synched up in a high-voltage lather of rhythmic palaver, taking no prisoners, and laying down metaphorical cadavers, white, *and* black. The revision is intra-communal as well as a weapon against the outside. But to focus solely on the word here is to miss what is most potent in the potential.

As this historically Afro-animated, Latino-levitated, Caribbean-rocked tradition of tagging reality with sound, sight, and youthful braggadocio has proliferated around the planet, what remains most identifiably hip-hoppish about it is the beat-in-the-body that serves as ground for the growing—and contradictory—repertoire of lyrical lambaste it leverages. In the States alone, it has become tool for transnational booty-call-profit-taking as well as underground pirating of party time, brutal gangsta bellicosity against criminal justice brutality and buppy felicity with upward mobility, conscious call for a new polity and skin-head hatred of all things dark. Overseas and south of the border, the mode goes recombinant and utterly promiscuous in both politics and theme. It may host Palestinian protest of Jewish imposition or Israeli abhorrence of Arab presence; Venezuelan celebration of Chavez's invocation of Cuban poet Marti's declamation, *Seamos moros!*, or Dominican Republican *reggaetón* porn, French-Arab *banlieues* rant against anti-Muslim discrimination and white French National Front anti-immigrant cant (Aidi, 43, 46, 48). The content is hardly determinative of the modality. But percussive rhyme and machine-gun rhythm are. The code is carried in a drummed up street-strut and corrosive tongue-cut that answers to hard concrete and heavy manners as its primary poetics of meat and gesture. No matter that its market-venue is 70% suburban in the ledgers of things countable in this country; its bootleg sharing is beyond numbering and clearly "ghetto" in bearing and swagger. However cross-racial in its posturing-*personas*-of-recognizable possession (Slim Shady mounting the head of Marshall Mathers as fed-up-advent of eminently marketable white-boy "dread"), hip-hop remains quintessentially "Afro" in comportment and elocution. Imani Perry describes its obvious and compelling transnational hybridity, multi-regional affinity, and creole originality as nonetheless unmistakably African American in aesthetic formation and political location, black in audience and conscious identification, ebonic and funked up in its get-down antiphony and bluesy[1] use of technology (Perry, 12–13, 20, 24). This is a local politics of assertion leveraging "black-speak" as an international Esperanto of the body and the beat.

Academic work on the aesthetic breakdown of capitalism's globalizing mono-culture can specify the precise configurations of sound production, body contortion, spray can manipulation and tongue inflection that contribute to alternative identity-construction among competing hip-hop communities across the country and the planet.

Adam Krims' *Rap Music and the Poetics of Identity,* for instance, offers intricate testament to a post-modern musical equivalent of modern visual art's "primitivist" uptake of Africanity after the turn of the 20th century (Krims, 2000, 1). In limiting itself to examination of commercially recorded "rap" music as a "media content" that is mass produced and distributed as popular culture (i.e., it does not focus on hip-hop culture in general, the underground, or so-called "authentic" or "resistant" scenes of reference), Krims' treatment augurs the degree to which global popular culture is now "haunted" by a sonic profile of grimace and aggression that closely resembles earlier avant-garde fascination with fetish-objects pirated from the mother-continent. The "impure product" Krims exegetes by no means loses its vernacular African American resonance when packaged as commercial-rap-hybrid, but does exhibit the degree to which a fan culture focus on the actual organization of the music embeds audience identity in sound poetics perhaps even more than other dimensions of the production (Krims, 2000, 3). A recent offshoot of this emphasis on musical construction is the "backspin"—against a two decade pre-eminence of the MC—of turn-tablist scratch modes ripping out new codes of identity outside older "homeboy" geographies, such as found in the battle-grounds of sound growing up around DJs like Honda of Japan or Qbert of the Bay Area Fil-Am (Filipino-American) community without an MC to split between them (Krims, 2000, 5).

But even when traffic reverses direction at the crossroads of global encounter with the local, the musical aesthetic remains subject to a critical judgment, listening for percussive clues that are substantially African in hue. Perhaps the epitome of this post-modern possession occurred when reality rap sandwiched dissonant pitch combinations and clashing timbral values into a sonic "assault-scape" incapable of representation or categorization by the Western-trained ear (Krims, 2000, 73). Such a "hip-hop sublime" finds one of its most outrageous signs in the 1990 Bomb Squad design of west coast rapper Ice Cube's first post-NWA record ("The N . . Ya Love to Hate" on *Amerikkka's Most Wanted* album) as some of the "illest" hardness on the street. But Krims is also prescient in tracing the compromising effects of the sonic menace thus delivered: the sublimity may ultimately sell out analysis to catharsis, mystifying rather than unmasking the economic forces actually producing ghetto devastation, by offering up the latter aurally as a form of titillation for white middle-class consumption (Krims, 2000, 74, 134; 2002, 70, 72).

When we move from sound composition to other dimensions of hip-hop expression, an art historian like Robert Farris Thompson can give precise delineation and formal genealogy to the mimetic reflections in gesture and dance that give somatic texture to the values of flow, layering, and rupture celebrated and explored in Tricia's Rose's *Black Noise* probe of the culture, including its visual register. Thompson's article entitled "Hip-Hop 101" unpacks the "body lightning" of both early east coast b-boy and b-girl styles and electric boogaloo west coast contributions to the cross-pollenization of five Afro-creole cultures, themselves beholden to even older dance vocabularies and spin-patterns deriving from Fula, Gelede, and Kongo traditions (Thompson, 211, 213, 218). Barbados, Jamaica, Cuba, Puerto Rico, and North America historically have brewed up an Afro-Latino-Anglo mix of moves that constitutes a veritable "zoo" of human dance innovation, not only signifying on ancestors, but "poppin'" and "tickin'" machine conniptions into humorous riffs on industrial ecology. Human mime of beatbox rhyme and pneumatic drill grinds combine into what we might call a synched up conga line of the off-timed body-mind. Thompson literally labels the volatility, "corporeal cubism" (Thompson, 219). Rose, on the other hand, divines the tri-partite aesthetic across all four hip-hop elements (Rose, 38). In graffiti, in particular, the layered-and-ruptured-flow grows out of the juxtaposition of a sweeping, curving script tripped by sudden breaks in the line alongside sharply angular letters tilted in "lean back" italics, with double and triple shadowing strobing the effect as an energy-riddle: a signified simultaneity of forces at once moving forward and backward, up and down, while exploding centripetally.

And even the MC tongue gets into the act in an inchoately Afro-suggestive form of attack. Here, the telling signature is not lyrical content, but the sonic hooks between the words. East Indian musician Russell Paul has offered yogic commentary on the clipped consonantal dexterities that animate word-smith lips on his web site. The chopped up mix of spit rhyme hints at an unconscious fix on what brahmanic tradition would articulate as mantric vibration and energy-release of the second or sexual *charka*-center (Paul, 1, 4–5). However the yogic illustration might play, the verbal action is unapologetically staccato—a vectored intervention into bodily habituation that aims at an erotic intensification of perception and movement. The formal element figured in this quick rundown as both quint- and non-essentially "African" can be glossed as "heightened contrast"—an apologetics of oppositional edginess provisionally incarnate in human habit as an "epistemology of the percussive," living by the impulse to vitalize energy by sharpening the differences between things, exploring the aesthetic qualities of Beauty by simultaneously auguring its integral other as the Great Erotic Ugly, a sophisticated existentialism of improvisation that a spiritual tradition like Haitian *voudoun* would underscore as the never-ending art of "balancing" reality, by intensifying its contrastive syncopations—Terror cheek-by-jowl with Desire.

Midnight time at the post-colonial crossroads

My subtitle is not mere poetics, but quite precise in its reference. In the early 20th century, a mask appeared, climbed out of an Iberian head on a squatting Picasso nude, leered in twisted grotesquery, dark, deformed, plumbing depths with an eye of macabre inquiry. And above, just as suddenly, another mask, possessing another pink-fleshed surface, breaking into the picture like a renegade dread, parting the drapery, parting seas, a face like a trumpet blowing, scarified in green opacities. And left, another Iberian head going native, Oceanic this time, staring at the apparitions across the tumbled space of the vision, trapping the two more nubile forms, arms akimbo over iconic hard gaze, pulling viewers in, pushing them out, breasts neither quite male nor female, planes of possible encounter neither open nor closed nor coordinated, a fractal forum, a world of pleasure and vertigo, brazen in confrontation of the spectral voyeur, the primitiveness orbing the prostitution like a global south breaking into the great white secret, eroticized, morbidized—a whole theater of colonial history and patriarchal misery throbbing with mystique, with rebuke, with horror. Feminist writer Anna Chave finds much amiss, here, much repeating from an old misogyny, but also laughs: the women hit back, with eyes, with angles, with take-no-prisoners, Medusa-headed terror; the clientele, the bordello-johns, the solicited soliciters offered gendered petrification, offered anger like a Matisse in his first viewing, or like the tittering of a Derain or Braque, not knowing how much they disclose in their uncomfortable guffaws (Chave, 263, 267, 271). Patron Uhde, in 1907, took, he says, weeks to recover, from his look. My own wife, Filipina former Methodist, mail-order academic, now post-colonial-scholar-on-the-rise, from out of prior evangelical fear at the figuration, today confesses attraction, pines tribal and summoned. *Demoiselles* is indeed icon, is for many fetish, mirror, a cathect-ion-vision from the down-under, born of projection. It is also primitivist and problematic, reinforcing stereotypes and war.

But whatever its late capitalist worth, its girth in the galleries of the art-elites of New York today, *Desmoiselles* marks a moment of mounting. And it hosts succession, offspring. Eminem is cousin to the gesture, four generations down the line. Modern art, the masters say, is primitivist to the core—recreating and perpetuating the "primitive" in the very act of valorizing its power. Across the Atlantic from Cubism's beginning, at century's end, hip-hop re-circulates the fantasy, giving sonic urgency to the grotesquery. Method Man's hosting of Buster Rhymes, zombie-eyed and spittin', in a bus straight out of the grave, ghetto-bound or erupting, is MTV-version of the same apparition. Or is it? Here, a *male* mirror of the male fear, pink flesh only "fronting" the cash behind the scene, becoming mere pixel, mere screen-body, while the commanding image goes all the way black, from doo-rag dome to the home of the foot on the chrome, at least in surface cast of the fetish. But just what is seen—what is the revelation that summons, the dark that so grips the white with biting desires, with fight and flight, with a flirtatious climb down? In the post-industrial possession of the popular culture mind, the throb of "the African" is not mere phantom, but a full-bodied eruption, penetration of drums, as well as stares, legs like helicopters, chopping the gaze, heads like drills, blazes of letters on skin as well as walls, sending architecture itself to tattoo school. Yes, possession is the right trope. Picasso was onto the real dope: it was exorcism, at least in vision; art, groping toward shamanic healing. But the collision he figured begs pause. There is a cause inside the confusion of his planes, a raw challenge inside the maw of the picture frame. And hip-hop works the same game, the same flame of painful possibility.

Those around Picasso who twigged to African potency saw only aesthetics, a felicitous or frightening new appearance of form, and tried simply to steal the show. Pablo, on the other hand, disdained (albeit untruthfully) mere appropriation, and on visit to the local Ethnography museum, fighting back horror amidst the dust and curatorial decrepitude, sensing something new, something very old, came unglued, heaved with a demon before the fetish-mask, discovered his vocation. Perhaps the closest he could get to vision quest, his gestalt hit him square in the pelvis, and he spent a lifetime, devoid of elders, trying to unpack the assault. But he knew it *as* assault, as apotropaic encounter with terror. And knew art as primarily, primordially, "weapon," amulet, objectified uncanny-ness, seeking mediation and redress for both desire and death. He had wrestled himself to the brink of this epiphany in solitude and austerity—quite a different surround from fetish-use in indigenous rites of shamanic passage—near suicide according to friends, expecting to find him noosed and gray one day, hanging behind his eight foot canvas. But this was only the beginning of the initiation, the first step out of the seduction of light, merely an inaugural kiss of the psychic midnight that would midwife magic letters like opaque graffiti from the primal face of objects.

By 1912, however, he had had a second encounter—this time with Grebo mask from the Ivory Coast—and broke through to recognition of the sign as utterly arbitrary and infinite inside a finite system of values: cowries, for instance, as an eye, or mouth, or navel, or vagina, or all of them at once, depending on the surrounding configuration; nails with equal possibilities given similar "sonorities." And more famously—definitively launching Cubism's shift from analysis to synthesis: cardboard and string as a guitar. The mask then was merely a basic contour; the perceived face—as shimmering revelation of volume "in front of" the material suggestion—was an effect of conjuration within a minimalist economy of signs (Bois, 91). This was "signifying" in the African American sense of the term, cubism as breakthrough of Eshu-Eleggua into Euro-pretense to control, the discovery of every signifier hovering, indeed convening, a crossroads of virtually infinite possibility within a space now open to other spaces, other signifieds and impurities. Saussure was discovering the same thing regarding language itself at the same time. This was not mere morphological fascination at work—Africa as novelty of (supposed) deformation and monstrosity—but rather what Picasso would call the *"raisonnable"* (the "reasonable") character of African sculpture (Bois, 74). Africa had long had a divine figure—and human practice—of such semiotic fecundity!

At the heart of the revelation—for Picasso as for Saussure—was the eruption of difference as constitutive of meaning. African art achieved its semiosis in the key of structural *abruption*: the juxtaposing of sharply contrasting discontinuities that provoked imaginative reconstitution along the lines of montage. This was an inkling of the universe as radically open—a freedom incubated ironically in a poetics of ever-proliferating and recombinant opposition. But not surprisingly, Picasso's cubist breakdown did not result in a send-up of either racist miscegenation or patriarchal domination. Surrealism and Ethnography, Feminism and post-colonial studies all to the good, we are here in a new century as mired in the binary absolutes of political opposition and economic asymmetry as ever. The primal masks topping the pink flesh in the *Desmoiselles* ensemble remain a cipher of the age. Western social structure has in no wise managed to move beyond fascinated terror before the numinous apparition to the free-wheeling creativity implied. Hip-hop now offers a global text of the same white (and indeed, black and other-colored) male conundrum. The issue remains exorcism, but "what haunts who" is a post-colonial ambivalence yet tethered in darkness, while midnight descends at the crossroads.

"Africa" climbing the spine like an unwanted mime

As emblematic gesture toward the requisite set of epiphanies and dislocations, I conclude with a bell hooks' riff on Jean-Michel Basquiat alongside Robert Linsley's Negritude reading of Wilfredo Lam. Both invoke possession—not in abstraction like a Picasso visiting the Trocadero sickness masks and recollecting in his studio, but specifically within sight of *voudoun's* historical experience. In the mix, Basquiat and Lam stand as structural similes to hip-hop's Afrophiliac advent in an artform now global in reach and pop in effect. As Afro-diasporic artists struggling against modernist assimilations of the deep black, both pay homage to Picasso's leverage even while themselves seeking to "possess" the Spaniard's syntax with another content.

Lam's ebony raid on *Desmoiselles* in his 1942 painting *The Jungle* offers piquant colonized commentary on the Picasso bordello—now set in a sugar-cane-surround, rounding out cubist flatness in Africanesque volume, hybridizing plants, animals, and people in a telling Surrealist gesture that also opens toward traditional shamanist shape-shifting (Linsley, 294). The tactic, says Linsley, is guerilla—an opportunistic seizure of *avant-garde* technique, opening a crack in the culture through which to initiate reverse trafficking, primitive colonizing European art, where the politics yet remained adamantine (Linsley, 194). Lam himself styles the strategy one of acting as a "Trojan horse that would spew forth hallucinating figures with the power to surprise, to disturb the dreams of the exploiters" (Fouchet, 188; Linsley, 293). If white power could not be brought to its knees militarily, at least get it flat on its back before Freud! Of course, in Cuba, the military victory did come, beleaguered and compromised as it was (as it was forced to be)—in the midst of which Lam's "ghoulish nocturnes" served as metaphors for the oppressive conditions under Battista, and his images of *voudoun* possession drawn from Santeria gave symbolic figurement to "Africa" erupting inside the social upheaval of revolutionary ex-slaves defying their colonial masters (Linsley, 300). Only post-revolution did Lam's occultism slide away from local politics toward a formalist virtuosity, more emblem of the problem than contestation of the condition.

Basquiat likewise soliloquizes the problem, penetrating the heart of whiteness to the bone, argues hooks, kneeling when necessary before the gallery masters and then making canvas yield the broken black aorta in the private spaces of his work (hooks, 343). Hooks reads the Haitian/Puerto-Rican-writer-on-the-"D"-train-walls in light of not only the white *avant-garde*, but Australian aboriginal x-ray painting and Maasai bone-speak (hooks, 343–344). Picasso-esque painting by way of serial destructions of the subject yields, in Basquiat's case, not the terrors of the colonial psycho-scape, but "the naked black image," dripping with blood (hooks, 343). Homage to the canon of Western beauty is paid in the coin of the gross deformity its hides: the Basquiat mask, clearly influenced by Picasso's vocabulary, is an unmasking, like *Desmoiselles* turned inside out. Here too, asserts hooks, the image is a wall of repulsion—an in-your-face repudiation of the gaze-that-seeks-only-seduction, commodification—a "primitive" up-take of modernism's primitivism to throw down an insider code, signing to *Obnoxious Liberals* (1982), "Not For Sale" even where it hangs with a price tag (hooks, 344). The impossible (black man) game of "fame" or "invisibility" in Jean-Michel's case is lost precisely in the winning: white critics are certain they know Basquiat's meanings, says hooks, almost exactly in proportion as they miss the pain signified (hooks, 346). hooks reads the results as "self-immolations"—as surely prophetic graffiti of white supremacy's ongoing effects as Basquiat's own early death repeats the SAMO-tale of black-male-unmaking before an impossible demand. The hooks cipher here is prescient. The terror in the mirror of these tags (even when they momentarily masquerade on SoHo walls) is not that of a disintegrating West, coming to the cataclysmic end of its history, but rather, hooks claims, dread of an unimagined space beyond imperial maleness (hooks, 348). This place, Basquiat—as indeed maleness in most of its historic heterosexual identifications, whatever the color—was unable to access beyond the phallocentric battleground (hooks, 347). What his paintings testify *to*, however, is black male agony in the complicity. It is the groan itself that gives glimpse of the possible "elsewhere."

And just here, hooks registers a faint hope (hooks, 349). Basquait's haunting minimalist figuration of a black-and-brown horseman mounted on white skeletal bones entitled *Riding with Death* (1988) evokes, in hooks, a possibility of possession that augurs healing. Possession here is not mere titillation, not simply modernist fascination with "primitive" visions of grotesquery, rifled for a momentary halt of male terror before castration and death. This is rather *voudoun* grasped as post-modern task: the (*avant-garde*) responsibility to employ trance to edge beyond the periphery of known boundaries, *and return unharmed* (hooks, 349, quoting Napier, 69). As anthropologist David Napier reports, unlike the case with some Western performance art, traditional trance travelers did not leave wounded bodies in their wake (Napier, 69). Possession could promise not just more sacrifice, but "recovery and return" outside the patriarchal stereotype and beyond the racial violence.

It is clear, as indicated in my opening for this writing, that a primitivist aesthetics is capable of conjuring both voice and vision beyond the interdictions of white male senility or identity. Picasso can provoke dementia to speak insight; Jay-Z or Beyonce may incite adolescent dreams of sacrificial giving. Over the course of a century, the grip of African form or ghetto beat has grabbed Western eyes and feet like a return of the repressed. But the sign has yet to be read all the way down. It is not simply the thug-ugliness of historic white sickness finding ironic comeuppance in a triumphant backspin of the art form. Yes, the suburb is penetrated by a dark grimace and a sonic penis against all parental guidance to the contrary. But the mirror has yet to be fathomed. What if the fetish is truth? Picasso's right-hand masks the left-hand demand of ritual maturation? Perhaps white male exorcism finds its complete evacuation only in possession by a prostitute-primitive hybrid, black mounting white like a recessive gene finding its bone, female-ferocity conjuring unclassifiable multiplicity from male anatomy? Perhaps the real antidote to the last 500 years of a planetary coping with Western-provoked genocide is a gay-lesbian trope of primitive energy probing the dope of blackface not as skin-tone, but as zone where all oppositions find their home and no possibility of roaming identity is left uncloned in parody or reality by digitalized dramaturgy? What if the signifying rhyme of hip-hop designs of polyrhythmic identity and graffitic insurgency and b-boy and girl bodily plasticity were pursued *that far*? And then the aesthetics is given a politics willing to die for its planetary rise?

Note

1. Cf. Houston Baker's elaboration of an analytic blues dynamic (in *Blues, Ideology, and African American Literature*) in the employment of found sounds like train whistles and track-clacks to give sonic representation to travel motifs and nomad grief in post-bellum America—a certain sensibility for the capacity of technology to give expression to themes of struggle and overcoming that, for Baker as for many others, is rooted in notions of musical notions of the "break."

Works cited

Aidi, Hisham, 2003, "Let Us Be Moors: Islam, Race and 'Connected Histories,'" *Middle East Report* 229, Winter, pp. 42–52.

Baker, Houston, 1984, *Blues, Ideology and Afro-American Literature*, Chicago: University of Chicago Press.

Bois, Yve-Alain, 1990, *Painting as Model*. Cambridge, MA & London: The MIT Press.

Chave, Anna C., 2002, "New Encounters with *Les Demoiselles d'Avignon*: Gender, Race, and the Origins of Cubism," in K. N. Pinder, ed., *Race-ing Art History: Critical Readings in Race and Art History*, New York: Routledge, pp. 261–87.

Fouchet, Max-Pol, 1976, *Wilfredo Lam*. New York: Rizzoli.

Gates, Henry Louis Jr, 1988, *The Signifying Monkey: A Theory of Afro-American Literary Criticism*, New York: Oxford University Press.

hooks, bell, 2002, "Altars of Sacrifice: Remembering Basquiat," in K. N. Pinder, ed., *Race-ing Art History: Critical Readings in Race and Art History*, New York: Routledge, pp. 341–9.

Jacob, Max, 1982, "Souvenirs sur Picasso contés par Max Jacob," in M. McCully, ed., *A Picasso Anthology: Documents, Criticism, Reminiscences*, Princeton, NJ: Princeton University Press, pp. 54–5.

Jung, Carl G. 1982, "Picasso," in M. McCully, ed., *A Picasso Anthology: Documents, Criticism, Reminiscences*, Princeton, NJ: Princeton University Press, pp. 182–6.

Kennedy, Randy, 2005, "The Pablo Picasso Alzheimer's Therapy," *New York Times* (October 30, 2005, 1D).

Krims, Adam, 2000, *Rap Music and the Poetics of Identity*, Cambridge: Cambridge University Press.

Krims, Adam, 2002, "The Hip-Hop Sublime as a Form of Commodification," in Regula Burckhardt Qureshi, ed., *Music and Marx: Ideas, Practice, Politics*, New York: Routledge, pp. 63–80.

Lindsley, Robert, 2002, "Wilfredo Lam: Painter of Negritude," in K. N. Pinder, ed., *Racing Art History: Critical Readings in Race and Art History*, New York: Routledge, pp. 289–306.

Napier, A. David, 1992, *Foreign Bodies: Performance, Art, and Symbolic Anthropology*, Berkeley: University of California Press.

Paul, Russill, 2002, "*About the Yoga of Sound*," http://www.russillpaul.com.

Perry, Imani, 2004, *Prophets of the Hood: Politics and Poetics in Hip Hop*, Durham, NC & London: Duke University Press.

Read, Herbert, 1959, *A Concise History of Modern Painting*, New York: Frederick A. Praeger, Inc.

Rose, Tricia, 1994, *Black Noise: Rap Music and Black Culture in Contemporary America*, Hanover, NH: Wesleyan University Press: Published by University Press of New England.

Salmon, André, 1982, "*La jeune peinture française*," in M. McCully, ed., *A Picasso Anthology: Documents, Criticism, Reminiscences*, Princeton, NJ: Princeton University Press, pp. 55–8.

Thompson, Robert Farris, 1996, "Hip Hop 101," in William E. Perkins, ed., *Droppin' Science: Critical Essays on Rap Music and Hip-Hop Culture*, Philadelphia: Temple University Press, pp. 211–9.

MICHAEL HARRINGTON AND THE "LEFT WING OF THE POSSIBLE"

Gary Dorrien

Nearly a hundred times per year for over thirty years, Michael Harrington heard himself introduced before he launched into an earnest, learned, humorous, sometimes rhetorically scintillating speech on some aspect of his democratic socialist politics. Gifted with charm and a quick wit, he was adept at handling hecklers; the low point of these events, from his perspective, usually came during the introduction. Nearly always he was described as "the author of *The Other America*, the book that sparked the War on Poverty," while his other books got short shrift. Harrington was too affable to admonish a welcoming host, but these introductions were hard to bear. Sometimes he reintroduced himself. "I've written quite a few books since *The Other America*, some of which might interest you," he would say. His major works were very important to him, and *The Other America* was not one of them. He could see his epitaph in the making: "Wrote *The Other America*, downhill after that."

That, indeed, is how Harrington is usually remembered. He usually gets a page or two in books on the Johnson administration and a brief mention in books on the Civil Rights movement, but as American socialism gets few books of any kind, the rest of his work is downgraded or forgotten. Even Maurice Isserman's otherwise splendid biography of Harrington, *The Other American*, says almost nothing about the aspect of his career that mattered most to him.[1]

Had Michael Harrington been born anywhere in Western Europe, he would have become a major social democratic party leader. Having been raised, instead, in Missouri, and then transplanted to New York, he could have become America's leading liberal political intellectual, but he was committed to building a serious social democratic tradition in his country. Thus, he settled for being America's leading socialist, which, as William F. Buckley Jr. once teased him from a podium, was something like being the tallest building in Kansas.

Edward Michael Harrington was born in St. Louis in 1928 to a securely middle-class family that was Irish Catholic on both sides. His father Edward Harrington was a mild-mannered patent lawyer whom Harrington described, in his writings and public interviews, as a gentle soul. His mother Catherine Harrington was a domineering personality whom Harrington described, with more reserve, as a "public-spirited" volunteer in Catholic and civic organizations. In private, Harrington explained that his mother was a militant Catholic whose dogmatism and forcefulness gave him much to overcome, though even to friends, he refrained from commenting on the irony of being an only child in a conservative Catholic household. Edward Harrington Sr. taught his son by word and example to do what Catherine wanted. After Harrington achieved fame for *The Other America*, Catherine recalled to an interviewer that when Michael was seven years old, "We were both reading in bed. He was reading Dickens and he turned to me and said, 'My, this author expresses himself well.'" That was a true picture, even if Catherine Harrington improved the quote.[2]

Michael Harrington was educated by the Jesuits at St. Louis University High School, where he was called Ned, and by the Jesuits at Holy Cross College, where friends called him Ed. At both places he was very young, having started high school at the age of twelve. Harrington later recalled that he grew up "in a pleasant Irish Catholic ghetto, which made the death of God particularly poignant for me." He also acknowledged that his training in Thomist scholasticism probably had something to do with his later attraction to Marxist scholasticism.[3]

After graduating from Holy Cross at the age of nineteen, near the top of his class, he took a few years to find himself. To please his parents, Harrington spent a year at Yale Law School, which bored him, and a year studying English at the University of Chicago, which he liked, but not enough to hang on for a doctorate. He later claimed that he converted from Taft Republicanism to Socialism near the end of his law schooling and that his "Damascus Road" conversion to social activism occurred during a summer job in St. Louis, where he worked for the public school system's Pupil Welfare Department. Standing in a decayed building that reeked of garbage, broken toilets, and overcrowded habitation, he recalled: "Suddenly the abstract and statistical and esthetic outrages I had reacted to at Yale and Chicago became real and personal and insistent. A few hours later, riding the Grand Avenue streetcar, I realized that somehow I must spend my life trying to obliterate that kind of house and to work with the people who lived there." Perhaps it did happen that way, as Harrington featured this story in both of his autobiographies. But Isserman could not find a Yale classmate who remembered him as a socialist, and Harrington worked for the Pupil Welfare Department for a total of three days.[4]

He started to become Michael Harrington on his next stop, Greenwich Village, where he aspired to become a socialist poet. Moving to New York in 1951, Harrington made his way to Dorothy Day's Catholic Worker House of Hospitality, in the Bowery, where he promptly took over the *Catholic Worker* newspaper and became a favorite of the founder. Although Harrington spent little time actually ministering to the poor—the newspaper proved more interesting—he repeated the Worker's standard answer to inquirers: He was there to become a saint. For nearly two years, he tried to adopt Day's anarcho-pacifist politics and her devotion to Catholic orthodoxy, while spending his evenings at the White Horse tavern, which was locally famous for the poets and writers who drank there—Dylan Thomas, Delmore Schwartz, Norman Mailer, William Styron and Dan Wakefield. Young Democratic Party operative Daniel Patrick Moynihan was another regular; for ten years Harrington was a fixture at the White Horse. He fancied himself a poet and Bohemian, smoked and drank every night, held court on politics and literature, took home many women, and dropped Day's anarchism, pacifism, and religion, in that order. Under the influence of a young operative in the Young People's Socialist League, Bogdan Denitch, Harrington joined the Socialist "movement," as YPSL cadre called their grouplet. Trading one unworldly sect for another, Harrington told himself that instead of merely ministering to human misery, he was working to abolish the system that produced it.

For twenty years he thrived in that world, outgrowing the youth section to become the eloquent golden boy of a quarrelsome, factional, New York Socialist environment, in Harrington's case as a Shachtmanite. Max Shachtman was a charismatic autodidact, party hack and orator who left his mark on a peculiar mixture of radicals and conservatives. He began his political pilgrimage as a communist and ended it as a father figure to the generation of right-wing Socialists and neoconservatives who won high positions in the Reagan Administration. In the 1920s, he was a Soviet-style Communist; in 1929 he cofounded American Trotskyism as a close associate of Leon Trotsky; in 1940 he founded the post-Trotskyist Independent Socialist League, which espoused what Shachtman called "Third Camp" revolutionary socialism; in the 1950s his theory of "democratic Marxism" provided the ideological scaffolding for democratic socialists who considered themselves too "hard" to be Norman Thomas Socialists; in the 1960s he moved to the right, joined the Socialist Party, and cozied up to the leadership of the AFL-CIO; subsequently he was revered by neoconservatives as a champion of militantly anticommunist trade unionism.

Harrington got his political education in the 1950s phase of the Shachtmanite school, which debated abstruse points of Marxist doctrine in sessions often lasting through the night. There were always rallies and "actions" to attend, but mostly, Shachtmanite socialism was about getting the arguments right. All of Harrington's comrades were Marxologists; he later described them as "determined, but unhysterical anticommunists engaged in seemingly Talmudic exegeses of the holy writ according to Karl Marx." From Shachtman, he inherited his signature theories of democratic Marxism and bureaucratic collectivism, as well as his socialist outrage at the communist perversion of socialism. Harrington recalled that when Shachtman gave one of his three-hour speeches on the evils of communism, reeling off the names of Socialist leaders murdered by Stalin, "it was like hearing the roll call of revolutionary martyrs who were bone of our bone, flesh of our flesh." This schooling in the intensely anticommunist faction of the Old Left shaped Harrington's early concept of the Socialist project and, in the early 1960s, undercut his relationships with youthful leaders of the New Left.[5]

In 1960, the non-youthful socialists of the League for Industrial Democracy (a Socialist youth-outreach vehicle with ties to the Shachtmanites and the Socialist Party) tried to regenerate their youth division by funding a new student organization later named Students for a Democratic Society (SDS). Harrington had spent the past two years lecturing at colleges and universities across the country, helping to build YPSL into a national organization boasting 1,000 members and a YPSL coalition project, the Student Peace Union, into a 10,000-member organization. He was the obvious choice to be the Old Left's bridge to the student generation. In early 1962 Harrington glowed when student movement leader Tom Hayden declared that his generation trusted only three people older than thirty: Norman Thomas, leftist sociologist C. Wright Mills, and Harrington. Hayden's fledgling protest organization, SDS, had a few hundred members at the time; Harrington set out to educate them about Left politics and building a serious student-based Left-wing movement.

But to Hayden, Al Haber, Richard Flacks, and other SDS leaders, YPSL was not a model of anything to emulate; meanwhile, Harrington could not resist lecturing them about things they didn't understand, owing to their deficient backgrounds in Left politics. YPSL specialized in factional disputes over fine points of ideological purity. Marxology prevailed, in the form of mimeographed, single-spaced position statements by rival caucuses. All of that repelled the SDS leaders. To them it was obvious that the American Left needed a different kind of student movement, one that dropped the Old Left's esoteric debates about Marxism and Socialism, its obsessive hatred of communism, and its nostalgic alliances with trade unions and Democratic Party liberalism.

In 1962, fifty-nine SDS delegates met at the United Automobile Workers camp in Port Huron, Michigan to draft a soon-famous manifesto, the Port Huron Statement, where they clashed with Harrington and YPSL leaders Richard Roman, Rochelle Horowitz, and Tom Kahn. The SDS leaders wanted to break free from anticommunism and the Democratic Party establishment; Harrington railed against them on both points. To him, making socialism American was paramount. Democratic socialism would never get anywhere in the United States, nor should it, if it was not militantly anticommunist and friendly to liberal democrats and unionists. To the SDS leaders, Harrington seemed obsessed with battles from another time and place. Making socialism American was not their cause; they took a low view of Socialism and a lower one of America. To them, anticommunism was simply the excuse that liberals and reactionaries used to justify the United States' wars and expanding military empire. Harrington later recalled, "My notion of a progressive, Leftist anti-Communist made as much existential sense to them as a purple cow." As liberals were part of the problem, the SDS took little interest in working with them: "They were in favor of political realignment, but dismissed the liberals who were essential to it."[6]

Briefly, at Harrington's urging, the League for Industrial Democracy cutoff funding for the SDS, an episode that grew with retelling in New Left lore. Harrington had been the youngest member of his high school class, his college class, his drinking gangs, and his socialist sects. Now he confronted younger student leaders who spurned his counsel, and he took it badly, damaging his reputation among young radicals just as they began to build a new left worth naming. It didn't help that he was right on the two main issues: The student radicals needed to recognize that communism was oppressive, murderous, and squalid, and that denigrating liberals was not the way to build a healthy progressive movement. But Harrington unnecessarily alienated the SDS leaders by talking down to them. He was too defensive about YPSL to acknowledge its repellent features, and the SDS leaders turned out to be perceptive about the upshot of his anticommunism. The Port Huron Statement acknowledged that Soviet Communism was ugly and oppressive; it also blasted the reigning Cold War militarism that turned the entire planet into an anticommunist battlefield. After Vietnam became the issue, Harrington took the wrong side nearly to the end of the 1960s, exactly as SDS expected.

Contrary to most accounts of this subject, however, Harrington never lost his access to most New Left leaders. He worked hard at rebuilding damaged relationships, and by the late 1960s he was well practiced at apologizing for his rift with the SDS, an apology he repeated on the lecture trail for the rest of his life. He regretted having botched his chance to influence the student movement. For the most part, he also resisted the "I told you so" mode after SDS degenerated into Maoist vanguardism and hooliganism. Self-righteousness was not Harrington's style, and he got better at confessing that his group missed its opportunity to bond with and restrain the New Left. More importantly, by the early 1970s he sorely regretted that it took him so long to oppose the Vietnam War. Harrington did not speak at an antiwar rally until October 1969, and he did not call for the United States to withdraw from Vietnam until January 1970.

Despite these regrets and mistakes, he connected with a large swath of the sixties generation as "the man who discovered poverty." *The Other America* gave Harrington an identity to a mass audience that knew nothing about Max Shachtman or even the Port Huron Statement. To a smaller number he also became the symbol of a humane, democratic socialist politics, even as many Leftists gagged on his anticommunism.

The Other America had inauspicious beginnings. As a professional activist, Harrington was adept at writing and speaking on topics he knew little about. In 1959, he knew a lot about communism, literary criticism, and civil liberties, his staple topics for *Commonweal* and *Dissent* magazines. About poverty he knew very little, aside from his brief experience at the Catholic Worker and occasional glimpses of urban poverty on his speaking tours. Liberal journals rarely mentioned poverty in the 1950s. To the extent that poverty still existed, liberals took it to be a marginal hangover, lacking any importance as a political issue. In 1959, most liberals believed that the basic structural problems of how government and business should work together had been solved. Economic growth would mop up residual "pockets of poverty" left over from the Depression. John Kenneth's Galbraith's *The Affluent Society* and Arthur Schlesinger, Jr.'s *The Vital Center* were the bibles of the new prosperity-liberalism. Although Galbraith later pleaded for a different reading of his celebrated book, it had perfect pitch for the Vital Center's blend of optimism and complacency.[7]

The Affluent Society brought out a few nay-sayers. Economist Leon Keyserling suggested that establishment liberalism might be too complacent by half. In 1958, noting that more than a quarter of American families reported annual incomes below $4,000, Keyserling suggested that there was a stronger case to be made for a new New Deal-style employment policy than Galbraith and Schlesinger let on. A few months later, Senator Paul Douglas of Illinois, in a speech published by the *New Leader,* called for a more aggressive government response to America's lingering poverty problem. *Commentary* editor Anatole Shub, sensing a hot topic, asked Harrington to write an article on poverty as a social and political issue.

Harrington was always a quick study. Using statistics from the Federal Reserve Board and the U.S. Commerce Department, he argued that

America had fifty million poor people. To explain how the affluent society of 1959 could still have that much poverty, he appropriated anthropologist Oscar Lewis' "culture of poverty" thesis: The problem was not mere unemployment and underemployment; rather, America's poor constituted "a separate culture, another nation, with its own way of life." This notion had a leftist spin in Lewis' and Harrington's usage, although in later years Harrington had to dissociate it from neoconservative usage, which employed the "culture of poverty" as a club to attack antipoverty programs. In a second article in 1960, on urban slums, he decried America's housing policy as cheap and lacking in compassion.[8]

Even Harrington did not regard poverty as a top priority issue, however. As an activist he gave first place to the Civil Rights Movement and second place to building a socialist movement; poverty was a secondary matter. By 1960, there were two full-fledged Civil Rights movements, which worked together, but operated differently. The northern movement was centered in New York, rooted in longstanding organizations, and professional in its structure and style. It handled fundraising and publicity for the movement as a whole, emphasized coalition building with sympathetic groups, and organized large national events such as the March on Washington. Harrington was a stalwart of this group of leaders and organizers, which included black socialists A. Philip Randolph, Bayard Rustin, and James Farmer. The southern movement grew out of the Montgomery Bus Boycott of 1955 and the student sit-ins of spring 1960. It was younger, less professional in style, structure, and ideology, and more radical tactically. Harrington shared the qualms of northern Civil Rights leaders about the expressive, theatrical style of the southern movement, but he also appreciated its advantages. Northern Civil Rights leaders were sometimes constrained by their institutions and professionalism, and they had to cope with the decline of an existing student movement. In the South, the movement was new and comparatively uninhibited, if ideologically undeveloped. As Harrington put it, "They came fresh to their rebellion." He treasured his friendships with Rustin and Martin Luther King Jr., often remarking that he knew from his first meeting with King in 1960 that King was a democratic socialist in all but name.[9]

Years later King enjoyed teasing Harrington about having discovered poverty. In the early 1960s, however, Civil Rights and socialism were consuming for Harrington, and he had no intention of turning his articles on poverty into a book, even after Edward R. Murrow's documentary, "Harvest of Shame," drew attention to the plight of migrant farm laborers. Harrington brushed off requests from publishers to write *The Other America*, until Macmillan offered a $500 advance, an enormous sum to a movement activist always pinched for bus fare. For it he wrote the book that changed his life.

The Other America explained that the land of the poor was invisible to middle-class Americans because it existed mostly in rural isolation and crowded urban slums. This America, its invisibility notwithstanding, numbered fifty million fellow citizens who belonged to a different society than the middle-class culture of affluence. It was also the product of social neglect: "Until these facts shame us, until they stir us to action, the other America will continue to exist, a monstrous example of needless suffering in the most advanced society in the world."[10]

Dwight Macdonald praised the book for forty pages in the *New Yorker*, setting off a flood of media attention and speaking requests for Harrington. The book became required reading for social scientists, government officials, student activists, and intellectuals. Economic adviser Walter Heller gave a copy to President Kennedy, who may have read it before ordering a federal war on poverty three days before his death. Shortly afterward Lyndon Johnson declared war on poverty, telling Heller that abolishing poverty was his kind of program. Johnson appointed Peace Corps director Sargent Shriver to head the new Office of Economic Opportunity, who appointed Harrington to the program's organizing group. Shriver briefed Harrington on the agency's mandate and budget, prompting Harrington to object that America would not abolish poverty by spending merely "nickels and dimes." Shriver archly replied, "Oh really, Mr. Harrington. I don't know about you, but this is the first time I've spent a billion dollars." That exchange, a staple of Harrington's subsequent lecture touring, explained for him why the United States lost its war on poverty. Government spending increased significantly between 1965 and 1968, he allowed, but that was to pay for the war in Vietnam and increases in Social Security and Medicare. The war on poverty got less than one percent of the federal budget.[11]

Harrington wore his fame uneasily. He could have used it as a ticket to individual stardom as a liberal—*The Other America* never mentioned socialism—but instead he promoted democratic socialism and tried to build new social democratic organizations. He could have written trade market bestsellers to boost his name and income—publishers pleaded for a sequel to *The Other America*—but he persisted in writing scholarly books on socialism and the crises of late-capitalism. He was a sensational speaker—expressive, flowing, charming, gifted at humorous asides, always making three well-outlined points—and he enjoyed his lecture touring. Yet in March 1965, while striding to a podium in San Diego, he nearly collapsed from the first blast of a nervous breakdown, which felt like a combination of vertigo and a heart attack.

At first he blamed his overcrowded lecture calendar and the stresses of the Civil Rights campaign; Harrington joined King a few days later in Montgomery, Alabama for the last day of the March from Selma. Later that spring he realized that he was not merely stressed out but violently depressed from repressed conflicts, for which he undertook four years of psychoanalytic treatment. As far as he could tell, parental influences aside, the culprit was his unexpected fame. It was absurd, to Harrington, that he became a minor celebrity by writing about poor people. He pretended that nothing had changed; he was still a servant of social justice causes, not a star who floated above them. But denial merely intensified the war within. For many years, long after he crawled out of denial, every time that Harrington walked to a podium he felt a flash of anxiety about another meltdown. He felt guilty about the money he earned from his lectures and books, he was embarrassed by the star treatment he received, and in 1979 he embarrassed many of his comrades by spending the money on a move to suburban Larchmont in Westchester County, for the sake of his wife and children, all the while lamenting that they suffered from his long lecture-touring absences.

When the activist organizations that Harrington subsequently founded garnered media attention, the spotlight nearly always fell on Harrington, for which he routinely apologized to the group. For much of his media coverage and many other observers, it was strange that Harrington wasted his time building up socialist organizations; obviously he could have risen higher without them. But Harrington never considered his organizational work optional; it was central to his identity as a socialist activist and intellectual. To him, the key decision of his life had to do with opting for the right kind of anticommunism.

In the late 1960s, Harrington agonized over Vietnam. His Shachtmanite comrades were mostly pro-war, but Harrington sympathized with Norman Thomas and other critics. He wanted to oppose the war, but was held back by the Old Left's embattled anticommunism and disgusted by the New Left's tendency to romanticize the Vietnamese revolution. He warned that the forced collectivization of North Vietnam offered a nasty preview of what a communist victory would look like in South Vietnam. Those who waved Vietcong flags had to ignore a great deal of North Vietnamese history: "They ignored, for instance, the fact that Ho Chi Minh had by his own admission carried out a bloody collectivization in the North over the dead bodies of some tens of thousands of 'his' peasants." Later he noted that those who disrupted peace rallies by waving Vietcong flags never tried out the same theatrics on less tolerant groups like the American Legion.[12]

In 1969, Harrington belatedly joined the antiwar movement, which set off an explosion in the Socialist Party. To many Old Left socialists and unionists, Harrington's conversion on Vietnam was a betrayal. Shachtman argued that the war should be judged on a political basis, not a moral one. What mattered was the political outcome—a communist victory. Harrington replied that America's intervention legitimized communism as a political force, effectively recruiting Vietnamese peasants to its ranks. It was too late to prevent the Vietnamese revolution from being overtaken by Stalinists as a response to popular resentment of French colonialism, the corruption of Vietnamese governments, and American imperialism, all of which the communists successfully exploited. American intervention gave propaganda victories to communists and secured their credibility as proponents of national liberation. Moreover, Harrington did not share the Shachtmanites' denigration of the moral issue or their revulsion for the American antiwar movement as a whole. He loathed the movement's pro-communist and vulgar anti-American sideshows, but judged that its mainstream had an ethical anti-imperialist basis.[13]

These disagreements played out in two successive conventions of the Socialist Party. At the 1972 convention Harrington listened incredulously as longtime friends declared their hope that Richard Nixon would smash George McGovern in the presidential election. For Harrington, that marked the sorry end of the party of Eugene Debs and

Norman Thomas. Leading a dissident faction out of the party, in 1973 he formed a new organization, the Democratic Socialist Organizing Committee (DSOC). Harrington was finished with the right-leaning Shachtmanites, but not the dream of building a vital democratic socialist movement.

To him and his friends at *Dissent* magazine, the phenomenon of socialists for Nixon deserved a name. Harrington reached for the term "neoconservative," a disputed label that stuck to Sidney Hook, Emanuel Muravchik, Arnold Beichman, Arch Puddington, John Roche, Bayard Rustin, Harry Overstreet, Carl Gershman, Rochelle Horowitz, Tom Kahn, Penn Kemble, Joshua Muravchik, and later, a sizable group of others including Irving Kristol, Midge Decter, Jeane Kirkpatrick, Michael Novak, Norman Podhoretz, Paul Wolfowitz, Richard Perle, and George Weigel. The neoconservatives derided the 'sixties generation of progressives as a "New Class" of self-seeking bureaucrats and opportunists. Harrington saw the same group as the hope of a new "conscience constituency" in American politics. He sought to bring together the McGovern wing of the Democratic Party, the social movements left over from the 'sixties, the progressive unions, and the progressive wing of the Socialist Party, urging that it was not to late to make socialism American.

Harrington's new group was more progressive and good-spirited than the one he left behind, but it was much less successful politically. Its early leaders included sociologist Bogdan Denitch, literary critic Irving Howe, school administrator Deborah Meier, union chief William Winpisinger, feminist icon Gloria Steinem, and Congressman Ron Dellums. DSOC worked primarily as a socialist caucus in the liberal wings of the trade union movement and the Democratic Party. It enjoyed strong support from the Machinists, Communications Workers, and American Federation of State, County and Municipal Employees, and in the mid- and late 1970s it made impressive inroads in the Democratic Party, especially at the national party's mid-term conventions. A further step toward healing and moving beyond the generational Old Left-New Left split occurred in 1982, when DSOC merged with a predominantly New Left organization, the New American Movement, to form Democratic Socialists of America. This merger brought feminist writer Barbara Ehrenreich, labor historian Stanley Aronowitz, and Black Studies scholar Manning Marable into the new organization and reversed the longstanding American socialist tradition of splintering into ever-smaller sects. Until his death in 1989, Harrington chaired or cochaired DSA, a "multi-tendency" group with as many greens and more feminists than the holdover reds from which it had come.

From the beginning, the band of battle-scarred progressive socialists that followed Harrington out of the Socialist Party strove to create a socialist organization that spurned ideological fanaticism, Cold War militarism, and, with substantial backsliding, male domination. From the mid-1970s on, DSOC mostly attracted members who knew and cared very little about the sectarian Old Left. Their frame of political reference had begun too recently to have a stake in the history of the Shachtmanites. They joined DSOC, or later, DSA, because they heard Harrington give an inspiring speech at their university. On occasion Harrington would make a scholastic point as an aside ("Here's a note for the Marxologists among you"), but generally he was careful to keep his sectarian Socialist past in the past. Some of his books rehashed Marxist debates at length, but not his campus lectures. He knew there was little in the Old Left to commend to young activists and he learned the hard way they were not interested anyway.

The eleven books that Harrington wrote after *The Other America* were terribly important to him, especially *Socialism* (1972), *The Twilight of Capitalism* (1976), *Decade of Decision* (1980), *The Next Left* (1986), and *Socialism: Past and Future* (1989). Most are forgotten now, and Isserman's biography barely mentions them, settling for a footnote that refers the reader to one of my early books and a monograph by Robert Gorman. This bifurcation of Harrington's life and thought underwrites the usual dismissal of Harrington's socialism, even if Isserman intended otherwise. Sociologist Alan Wolfe typifies the usual dismissal, declaring that Harrington's books after *The Other America* were failures "because Harrington was too busy fighting forgotten battles to concentrate on the writing of them." Harrington kept plugging for democratic socialism long after he should have gotten his clock fixed.[14]

To some degree, Wolfe is certainly right; whether he is wholly right depends on one's politics. Among the "forgotten battles" that Harrington might better have let go was his persistent defense of Karl Marx, to which he devoted his two major mid-career works, *Socialism* and *The Twilight of Capitalism*. In essence, Harrington argued that Marx was a democratic socialist very much like Harrington. Old fixations were hard to break; Harrington had to have Marx on his side, even if that blocked the view of Harrington's thoroughly democratic and freedom-supporting socialism. Harrington claimed that the real Marx was a "foe of every dogma, champion of human freedom and democratic socialism." Marx wrote some things that gave a very different impression, Harrington allowed, but the bad parts of Marx were temporary lapses, and Frederick Engels compounded the problem with his unfortunate invention, dialectical materialism.[15]

In Harrington's rendering, the *Communist Manifesto* featured a "schizophrenic" exaggeration of capitalist achievements and communist promise. Its opening line, that the "specter of communism" haunted Europe, was absurd, since Europe in 1848 was at war over bourgeois freedoms, not communism. Marx and Engels knew they were blowing smoke, Harrington argued. In section two, they announced the funeral of the bourgeoisie, but in the final section they advocated an alliance with it. Marx furiously denounced the bourgeoisie while trying to bring it to power. Harrington explained the contradiction by granting Marx a weakness for dramatic motivational language. Marx's specter and funeral language was obviously premature; thus he advocated tactical alliances with Chartists in England, agrarian reformers in the United States, petty-bourgeois radicals in France, and the bourgeoisie itself in Germany.[16]

But what kinds of alliances did he want? Near the end of the manifesto Marx contended that the bourgeoisie was fundamentally hostile to proletarian interests and in Germany the bourgeois revolution would be the "immediate prelude" to a proletarian revolution. That sounded like Leninism: an immediate transition from a bourgeois to a communist revolution, skipping an intervening period of bourgeois government. Was Leninism Marxist? Harrington urged that instead of taking Marx's "immediate prelude" statement literally, it was better to understand Marx by what he did in 1848, advocating long-term alliances with bourgeois democrats. But that was not much of a difference, because only a few months later, still in 1848, Marx urged workers to form secret armed organizations that prepared for immediate class war. And in 1850, he urged workers to set up revolutionary proletarian regimes alongside the victorious bourgeois governments, for "from the very first moment of the victory, the workers must distrust not only the defeated reactionary party, but its former comrades as well, and fight that party which will try to exploit the common victory on its own."[17]

Harrington used a stage theory to dispose of these counterfactuals, explaining that the bad Marx prevailed between 1849 and 1850. For two years Marx was an ultra-Leftist who envisioned the proletarian revolution as a popular explosion or insurrection from below. But even during Marx's bad phase, Harrington argued, he was a Jacobin democrat, never a Leninist. Marx advocated independent revolutionary regimes to stoke popular explosions, not vanguard dictatorships that deceitfully manipulated the proletariat or conspired coups. Admittedly, on several occasions during this phase Marx used the fateful phrase, "dictatorship of the proletariat." In April 1850 he and Engels signed the declaration of the World Society of Revolutionary Communists, which announced: "The aim of the association is the overthrow of all privileged classes, their subjugation by the dictatorship of the proletariat which will maintain the revolution in permanence until communism, the last organizational form of the human family, will be constructed."[18]

Harrington dealt with the latter problem by invoking the early Sidney Hook's explanation that Marx had a peculiar understanding of dictatorship. For Marx, Hook explained in 1933, "dictatorship" referred to the class basis of pre-communist societies, not revolutionary repression. Every state was a dictatorship, including the bourgeois democracies, because the purpose of the state was to uphold the economic and political power of the ruling class. Marx believed that the state was necessary only in class societies, to uphold and defend class privileges. Once the proletarian revolution overthrew capitalism and smashed the capitalist state, the state would not be necessary; a communist state was a contradiction in terms. Even revolutionary states were dictatorships in this sense of the term. Marx described the Paris Commune as a dictatorship because its property forms organized a proletarian form of class rule; it favored the working class over the bourgeoisie. Establishing revolutionary governments was never really the point for him, Harrington argued, following Hook; neither was repressing civil liberties. For Marx the point was for a revolutionary majority to overthrow capitalism and set up a government favoring its own interests. Then, the revolution would abolish the state too.[19]

That was a plausible exegesis, but it did not exactly advance Harrington's purpose of making Marxism attractive to Americans. In the Marxist sense, Harrington argued, a dictatorship brought about the fulfillment of democracy. Just as the triumph of the bourgeois revolutions brought about gains in civil liberty, the proletarian revolution brought about the fulfillment of economic freedom. Marx's example was the Paris Commune, a failed insurrection of city workers. Although a fiasco, Marx defended it forcefully. In the Paris Commune, all official jobs of all levels were paid the same wages as workers received, and all administrative, judicial, and educational officers were elected and recallable by universal suffrage. To Marx that was a model of proletarian dictatorship as democracy; Harrington contended that Marx advocated dictatorship only in this sense, as the fulfillment of democracy.

But Marx's faith in the withering away of the state under communism was utopian and stupendously destructive; he was never a good democrat in the sense of practicing humane democratic values; and at times he resorted to violent tactics and vicious rhetoric that flunked minimal tests of democratic principle. He flirted with the vanguard conspiracy theories of Louis Auguste Blanqui, called for massive insurrections from below, advocated secret societies, and repeatedly skewered opponents, factional rivals, and hapless followers with violent invective, calling them "toads," "vermin," "the emigrant scum," and the like. His violent exhortations to take up revolutionary violence are very hard to construe as democratic, especially as the proletarian movement was pitifully small and disorganized in the late 1840s. Moreover, Marx kept calling for the dictatorship of the proletariat well after passing through his ultra-left phase. In 1852, he told Joseph Weydemeyer that his central discovery was the structural development of the class struggle, which "necessarily leads to the dictatorship of the proletariat," and that "this dictatorship itself only constitutes the transition to the abolition of all classes and to a classless society." That formulation combined the three planks of what came to be called "vulgar Marxism": determinism, the dictatorship of the proletariat, and utopianism.[20]

When Harrington was not writing about Marx, he was a staunch opponent of revolutionary utopianism. Repeatedly, he repudiated the utopian impulse as incipiently totalitarian. Yet he passed over the rather large problem of utopianism in Marx's thought with a quick assurance and dismissal. In *The German Ideology* Marx fantasized that under communism, because general production would be regulated by society, it would be possible for a worker "to do one thing today and another tomorrow, to hunt in the morning, fish in the afternoon, rear cattle in the evening, criticize after dinner, just as I have a mind, without ever becoming hunter, fisherman, cowherd, or critic." Marx dropped the lyricism in his later career, but not his faith in the classless and stateless utopia. His anarcho-syndicalist idea of communism was pure utopianism and his last word on the subject. He had no theory of the revolutionary state beyond the promise of withering away. Marx put it plainly in his 1874 review of Bakunin's *Statism and Anarchy:* "When class rule has disappeared, there will no longer be any state in the present political sense of the word." Communism meant self-government for all; when the revolution brought about collective property and the abolition of classes, "the so-called will of the people disappears in order to make way for the real will of the co-operative."[21]

Marx actually believed that a proletarian revolution would abolish class domination and therefore the need for a political state. This was hardly a minor aspect of his thought, but Harrington brushed it aside as a negligible slip-up. In the twentieth century, he assured, "Marxism must be more chastened, but not less militant." Similarly, Harrington claimed that Marx was not an economic determinist, except on occasions when he was "unjust to his ideas." Marx's Preface to the *Critique of Political Economy* (1859) was a notable example: "The mode of production determines the social, political, and spiritual life processes in general." That was clear enough, but Marx amplified: "It is not the consciousness of men that determines their existence but, on the contrary, their social existence determines their consciousness." All intellectual, political, and religious phenomena were superstructural rationalizations of economic interests. In Harrington's view, this formulation fell under the rule, "Even Homer nods." The real Marx was not the economic determinist of the Preface, but the antimechanistic Hegelian of the *Grundrisse* who taught that the economic, political, and cultural dimensions of society interact and mutually determine each other.[22]

Harrington was surely right that Marx, a thinker of enormous power, was more sophisticated than vulgar Marxism and that the preface to the *Critique of Political Economy* oversimplified his argument by trying to summarize it concisely. But here the rule of watching what Marx actually did is instructive. Marx published the preface, stood by it, repeated it in other contexts, and republished it; meanwhile he did not publish the *Grundrisse*. Had he shared Harrington's concern to absolve Marxism of economic determinism, he would not have disseminated and recycled his formulation about it so determinedly, which supported his concept of class. Harrington did not believe that the mode of production determined the organization of slave and feudal societies, but Marx did believe it. For him, a class was defined precisely by its function in the mode of production; thus, as he declared in the *Communist Manifesto,* "the history of all hitherto existing society is the history of class struggles."[23]

In Harrington's telling, Marx was a sophisticated social scientist who tolerated Engels' vulgar Marxism out of loyalty to him and because Engels accepted the disagreeable task of defending Marx/Engels from their critics, especially German Socialist rival Karl Eugen Dühring. Engels promoted a crude base-superstructure theory that popularized Marxism, with unfortunate results. But Harrington wrongly played down Marx's role in developing the Marxist tradition. Besides being a sophisticated social scientist, Marx was a revolutionist who read and approved the entire manuscript of Engels' *Anti-Dühring* and even wrote one of its chapters. Marx did not get a reputation for economic determinism only because he tolerated Engels' defense of him. He wrote and promoted the works that shaped the Marxist tradition on this issue. Harrington was certainly right that Marx's totalitarian "followers" distorted and abused his thought. To Marx, communist transformations were possible only in industrialized societies that had gone through capitalist accumulation; moreover, it was a terrible irony of history that "Marxism" came to be associated with repugnant forms of state collectivism. But Marx's utopianism, determinism, rhetorical violence, and advocacy of secret societies and vanguard strategies all had something to do with that outcome.

Harrington's sensibility and vision were vastly better than Marx's. Sadly, he burned too much time and effort trying to convince readers that Marx shared his politics. He made better use of the theory of bureaucratic collectivism, which he always attributed to Shachtman. The idea of bureaucratic collectivism originated as an attempt to explain what went wrong in the Soviet Union. As early as the mid-1920s, Marxists and anarchists—some of them in Stalin's concentration camps—began to refer to the Soviet system as a state capitalist regime run by a "New Class" of professional bureaucrats. Christian Rakovsky, drawing on the pre-Bolshevik anarchism of Michael Bakunin, Peter Kropotkin, and Waclaw Machajski, described the Soviet leadership as a New Class of dictators whose rule was based on a new type of private property: collectivist state power. In the 1930s, the theory of the New Class was refashioned by American Trotskyists James Burnham, Joseph Carter and Max Shachtman, and Italian Trotskyist fellow-traveler Bruno Rizzi, all in opposition to Leon Trotsky.[24]

Trotsky contended that the Soviet regime—a degenerated workers' state under Stalin—would either move forward to socialism or backward to capitalism. At the founding congress of the Socialist Workers Party in 1937, however, Burnham and Carter challenged this premise, arguing that the Soviet regime was taking on a viable structure of its own. It was not a bourgeois state degenerating into outright capitalism *or* a workers' state moving forward to socialism, but something else, a bureaucratic deformation of a workers' state. In the factional Trotskyist debates of the later 1930s, Burnham and Shachtman argued that the traditional definition of a class did not cover the new form of social organization invented in the Soviet Union. Shachtman put it bluntly: "What we have called the consummated usurpation of power by the Stalinist bureaucracy was, in reality, nothing but the self-realization of the bureaucracy as a class and its seizure of state power from the proletariat, the establishment of its own state power and its own rule." Before the Bolshevik revolution, Trotsky warned that merely socializing poverty in a backward nation would never create a workers' state; to succeed, the Bolshevik revolution would have to depend on the aid of the international proletariat. But the Bolsheviks were left on their own, Shachtman explained, and the workers' state *was* overthrown, though not by a bourgeois restoration. The Soviet regime amounted to a new kind of counterrevolutionary class: "The old crap was revived in a new, unprecedented, hitherto unknown form, the rule of a new bureaucratic class."[25]

When the state takes over the means of production, the question changes to, "Who owns the state?" That question eventually drove Shachtman, after a prolonged bout with quasi-Trotskyism, to a form of democratic state socialism. The only true workers' state had to be democratically owned and controlled by workers, he argued. Soviet

Communism had no place in the history of Socialism, because democracy was the essence of Socialism. Just as the defining feature of capitalism was private ownership and the defining feature of communism was totalitarian ownership, the defining feature of socialism was democratic ownership and control. Having cofounded American Trotskyism in 1929, Shachtman was compelled by the first glimmerings of this conclusion to start over, forming a new Workers Party in 1940 (originality in nomenclature was little known in these circles), which later morphed into the Independent Socialist League (where he became Harrington's mentor), which he later led into the Socialist Party, where he became a Right-wing Socialist and guru to the original neoconservatives.[26]

Harrington's major works featured the idea of bureaucratic collectivism as a critique of late capitalism. For him the serious question was not whether economic planning would take place in the future, but the form in which it would take place. Corporate capitalism was increasingly a top-down form of bureaucratic collectivism in which huge oligopolies administered prices, controlled the politics of investment, bought off the political system, and defined cultural tastes and values while obtaining protection and support from the state, Harrington argued. It shook down the state for subsidies and favors and was happy to socialize its losses with government bailouts, but preached private enterprise and the right to free capital flows when its profits were questioned. Most importantly, capitalism granted control over investment, credit and social planning to unelected elites holding quite particular interests in the increase of their own wealth and power. It was fine to bail out too-big-to-fail capitalist enterprises with public money, as long as the public interest got no stake in the companies.[27]

For Harrington, democratic socialism was essentially a vision of an alternative future in which an inevitably collectivized society was effectively democratized. It had almost nothing to do with economic nationalization and everything to do with economic democracy. The mission of democratic socialism was to democratize the collectivist logic of modernity. In 1986 he put it bluntly: "The issue of the twenty-first century and of the late twentieth century is, can that collective tendency be made democratic and responsible? Can it be made compatible with freedom?" He believed that freedom would survive the ascendance of globalized markets and corporations only if it took the form of decentralized economic democracy. Harrington opposed economic nationalization on both philosophical and programmatic grounds. Unlike state socialism, corporate capitalism, and other forms of authoritarian collectivism, Harrington-style economic democracy promoted decentralized worker and community ownership and regionally based economic planning. In the 1970s and 1980s, his vision got greener and more insistent on human-scale community forms of socialization, ratcheting down the economism of his Old Left past. On the lecture trail, he was fond of admonishing Old Leftists that "any idiot can nationalize a bank," which became his judgment on France's bank nationalizations of the 1980s. To some comrades and critics that smacked of selling out socialism; Harrington replied: "To think that 'socialization' is a panacea is to ignore the socialist history of the twentieth century, including the experience of France under Mitterrand. I am for worker- and community-controlled ownership and for an immediate and practical program for full employment which approximates as much of that ideal as possible. No more. No less."[28]

For Harrington, the purpose of democratic socialism was to empower ordinary people and thus preserve and extend democratic freedom. He pointed to public bank models, such as the Meidner Plan for Economic Democracy in Sweden, and other experiments in worker and social ownership as examples of the decentralized democratic socialism of the future. Democratic empowerment was the prize, which an increasingly global, predatory capitalism devoured: "I would argue that the bureaucratizers, the collectivizers, the anti-freedom tendencies of modern society are the corporate capitalist tendencies of late capitalism, and that the alternative of freedom is represented by the democratic socialist movement for which I speak."[29]

Harrington took very seriously the necessity of believing in ordinary people and his own moral obligation to inspire hope. Often he told campus audiences: "If you consider your country capable of democratic socialism, you must do two things. First you must deeply love and trust your country. You must sense the dignity and humanity of the people who survive and grow within your country despite the injustices of its system. And second, you must recognize that the social vision to which you are committing yourself will never be fulfilled in your lifetime." That was a far cry from the party of Debs and Thomas, which promised "Socialism in our time" even when it knew better. After the lecture was over and Heineken time had commenced at a local hotel bar, Harrington could be bleak about where history was going. He hated the kind of Leftism that paraded self-righteous superiority and tagged every opponent as a "fascist," but in private he would allow that the emerging system of global corporate giants wedded to pliant governments was "a kind of fascism."

His last book, *Socialism: Past and Future*, expounded his "visionary gradualist" strategy, which conceived democratic socialism as a stubborn, persistently reformist pressure for further gains toward democratic self-determination: "I insist that the political, social, and economic development of modern society points socialism toward an ethical, multiclass, and decentralized conception of its goal based on the democratization of the workplace and the creation of new forms of community, both within and throughout the world. That vision has a remarkable continuity with the basic republican values that derive from both the French and the American revolutions." Harrington understood very well how far that was from Marx, although he insisted that the core of his vision was still Marxist. In his closing paragraph, he declared that if the socialist movement could learn from the failures of its past about how to create the future, "then there is hope for freedom, solidarity, and justice. And perhaps there will be a visionary gradualism equal to the challenge of the 'slow apocalypse' in which we live."[30]

In my introduction to this book, I noted that religion gnawed at Harrington. As a reasonably good Marxist, Harrington believed that religion was passing into oblivion, but he also worried that the passing of legitimizing religious authority left Western societies without a moral basis to inspire virtue or define common values. He proposed that the job of providing a legitimizing, integrating principle of Western culture should be taken up by democratic socialism. Specifically, in *The Politics at God's Funeral* he called for a new "united front" of religious and secular socialists to redeem the values of religious socialism and fill the void left by terminal Western religions. The new socialist united front would recover the values of progressive Judaism and Christianity, he wrote, "but not in religious form." It would require religious activists to subordinate their religious concerns to the needs of the movement to promote the values it held in common with other socialists. Harrington believed that progressive religious values would survive without religion and he assumed that religion was dying anyway. Socialism was a vehicle to keep progressive religious values alive.[31]

"But Mike," I would say, "what if religion isn't dying after all? What if the survival of religion is far more certain than that of socialism? And what if the movement that you want needs living, vital religious currents to sustain itself?" Mike didn't like these questions, so he usually changed the subject or shifted to scholastic points about philosophers and theologians. But he was an example of the possibility that he hoped for. Although not a religious believer, Harrington *was* religiously musical, and deeply influenced by Christian ethical teaching. He welcomed and respected religious comrades, and his organizations had quite a few of them, most notably Cornel West, Rosemary Radford Ruether, and Michael Eric Dyson.

Harrington had a tendency to substitute belief in Marx for his loss of religious belief, but the list of Marxist notions that he disbelieved got longer with age. He could hear the ghost of Marx ridiculing his "visionary gradualist" politics as a revival of the utopian socialism that Marx ridiculed in the 1840s. But the failures of twentieth century "socialisms" bearing Marx's name undercut the force of this criticism. Socialism was no longer innocent and could not afford to ignore Marx's mistakes. Marx mistook the rise of capitalism for its decline and mistakenly assumed that the middle-classes in industrialized societies would become proletarianized. Worse yet, his revolutionary utopianism made it possible for generations of totalitarian thugs to call themselves Marxists. Harrington said all of this plainly in his last years, without disavowing his conviction that democratic Marxism was the last best hope of humankind.

He died of cancer in 1989, carrying on until the end with a full calendar of lectures, organizing, and writing. Irving Howe later remarked that Harrington's gentleness seemed almost a flaw. There was not a trace of meanness in him; he lacked the hardness of the typical political leader and was thus extremely reluctant ever to criticize a comrade. Near the end of his life, after one of my books strongly criticized some of Harrington's arguments, I waited anxiously for his reaction. "So you think I don't know how to read Marx, do you?" he teased. "Well, you're in good company." He relinquished the hope of ever straightening out people like me. But what delighted him in his last years, he said, was that he finally belonged to a Left organization in which people could criticize each other without generating destructive intrigues, factional schisms, and personal attacks.

That was, in large part, his personal achievement. It is not only the left that is poorer today for having no one like him. American politics as a whole is poorer. Bill Clinton's presidency suffered from lacking a strong progressive flank in his party compelling him to do something about inequality, energy, and health care. Lacking any ballast on the left, Clinton's triangulating politics predictably tilted away from core progressive concerns. Whatever illusions Harrington may have indulged on other subjects, he would have understood very keenly that Clinton needed a strong left flank, and that Barack Obama needs one now.

Notes

1. This chapter adapts material from Gary Dorrien, "The Other American," *Christian Century* (October 11, 2000); and Dorrien, *The Democratic Socialist Vision* (Totowa, NJ: Rowman & Littlefield, 1986), 98–135; see Maurice Isserman, *The Other American: The Life of Michael Harrington* (New York: Public Affairs, 2000).
2. Michael Harrington, *Fragments of the Century* (New York: Saturday Review Press, 1973), 1; Harrington, *The Other America: Poverty in the United States* (1962; New York: Macmillan, 1993), v; Marion Magid, "The Man Who Discovered Poverty," *New York Herald Tribune Magazine* (December 27, 1964), 9; "Once Known for Her Own Record, Now She Is Michael's Mother," *St. Louis Post-Dispatch* (January 20, 1971), quote cited in Isserman, *The Other American: The Life of Michael Harrington*, 9–14, quote 12.
3. Harrington, *Fragments of the Century*, 71–77, quote 1.
4. Ibid., quote 66; Michael Harrington, *The Long-Distance Runner: An Autobiography* (New York: Henry Holt, 1988), 1; Isserman, *The Other American: The Life of Michael Harrington*, 54–55.
5. Harrington, *Fragments of the Century*, quotes 76, 77.
6. Ibid., quotes, 145, 147.
7. John Kenneth Galbraith, *The Affluent Society* (Boston: Houghton Mifflin, 1958); see Arthur Schlesinger, Jr., "The Challenge of Abundance," *The Reporter* (May 3, 1956), 8–11.
8. Michael Harrington, "Our Fifty Million Poor," *Commentary* 28 (July 1959), 19–27; Harrington, "Slums, Old and New," *Commentary* (August 1960), 118–124; Oscar Lewis, *Five Families: Mexican Case Studies in the Culture of Poverty* (New York: Basic Books, 1959); Isserman, *The Other American: The Life of Michael Harrington*, 175–220.
9. Michael Harrington, "Notes on the Left," *New Leader* 44 (May 22, 1961), quote 17; see Harrington, "The Economics of Racism," *Commonweal* 74 (July 7, 1961), 367–370.
10. Harrington, *The Other America*, quote 191.
11. Here as elsewhere in this chapter I am drawing from memories of things I heard Harrington say numerous times.
12. Michael Harrington, *Socialism* (New York: Saturday Review Press, 1972), quote 211; Harrington's *Village Voice* articles of this period are reprinted in Harrington, *Taking Sides: The Education of a Militant Mind* (New York: Holt, Rinehart and Winston, 1985), 101–136.

13. Max Shachtman, et al., "Statement on Vietnam," *Hammer & Tongs* (October 9, 1970), 8; Michael Harrington, "The Vietnam Moratorium," *New America* (October 25, 1969), 2; Harrington, "Getting Out of Vietnam," *Dissent* 17 (January–February 1970), 6–7.
14. Alan Wolfe, review of *The Other American: The Life of Michael Harrington*, by Maurice Isserman, *The New Republic* (April 3, 2000), 34–37; see Robert A. Gorman, *Michael Harrington: Speaking American* (New York: Routledge, 1995).
15. Harrington, *Socialism*, 29–108; Michael Harrington, *The Twilight of Capitalism* (New York: Simon and Schuster, 1976); quote 5.
16. Harrington, *Socialism*, 36–45; Karl Marx and Frederick Engels, *The Communist Manifesto* (1848), reprinted in *Karl Marx: Selected Writings*, ed. David McLellan (Oxford: Oxford University Press, 1977), 221–247.
17. Marx and Engels, *The Communist Manifesto*, 246; Harrington, *Socialism*, 45–49, quote 49; see Karl Marx, "Address to the Communist League," *Karl Marx: Selected Writings*, 277–285; Marx, "Speech to the Central Committee of the Communist League," *Karl Marx: Selected Writings*, 298–299.
18. Harrington, *Socialism*, 50.
19. Ibid., 50–52; Sidney Hook, *Towards the Understanding of Karl Marx: A Revolutionary Interpretation* (New York: John Day, 1933).
20. Karl Marx to Joseph Weydemeyer (March 5, 1852), *Karl Marx: Selected Writings*, 341.
21. Karl Marx and Frederick Engels, *The German Ideology* (1844), *Karl Marx: Selected Writings*, 159–191, quote 169; Karl Marx, "On Bakunin's State and Anarchy," (1874), *Karl Marx: Selected Writings*, 562–563.
22. Harrington, *The Twilight of Capitalism*, quotes 183, 42; Karl Marx, Preface to *A Critique of Political Economy*; *Karl Marx: Selected Writings*, 388–391; Marx, *Grundrisse*; *Karl Marx: Selected Writings*, 345–387.
23. Marx, *The Communist Manifesto*, 222.
24. See Bruno Rizzi, *The Bureaucratization of the World*, trans. Adam Westoby (1939; reprint, New York: Free Press, 1985); Max Nomad, *Rebels and Renegades* (1932, reprint, Freeport, NY: Books for Libraries Press, 1968); Nomad, *Apostles of Revolution* (1939, reprint, New York: Collier Books, 1961).
25. Max Shachtman, untitled essay written in 1940, reprinted in Shachtman, *Bureaucratic Revolution: The Rise of the Stalinist State* (New York: Ronald Press, 1962); also reprinted under the title "Stalinism: A New Social Order," *Essential Works of Socialism*, ed. Irving Howe (New Haven: Yale University Press, 1976), 526–546; see Leon Trotsky, "Socialism in a Separate Country?" Appendix 2, Trotsky, *The History of the Russian Revolution*, trans. Max Eastman (1932, reprint, New York: Monad Press, 1980), 378–418; Leon Trotsky, "A Letter to Max Shachtman," Trotsky, *In Defense of Marxism: Against the Petty-Bourgeois Opposition* (New York: Merit Publishers, 1965), 37–41.
26. See Julius Jacobson, "The Two Deaths of Max Shachtman," *New Politics* 10 (Winter 1973), 96–99; Tom Kahn, "Max Shachtman: His Ideals and His Movement," *New America* 10 (November 16, 1972), 5; Irving Howe, *A Margin of Hope: An Intellectual Autobiography* (New York: Harcourt Brace Jovanovich, 1982), 40–55; Harrington, *Fragments of the Century*, 67–75; Maurice Isserman, *If I Had a Hammer...The Death of the Old Left and the Birth of the New Left* (New York: Basic Books, 1987), 37–75.

27. Harrington, *Decade of Decision: The Crisis of the American System* (New York: Simon and Schuster, 1980); Harrington, *The Next Left: The History of a Future* (New York: Henry Holt, 1986); Harrington, *Socialism: Past and Future* (New York: Arcade Publishing, 1989).
28. Michael Harrington, "Harrington Replies," *The Nation* (June 14, 1986), 3.
29. Michael Harrington, "Is Capitalism Still Viable?" *Journal of Business Ethics* 1 (Dordrecht, Holland and Boston: D. Reidel Publishing Company, 1982), quote 283.
30. Harrington, *Socialism: Past and Future*, 277, 278.
31. Michael Harrington, *The Politics at God's Funeral: The Spiritual Crisis of Western Civilization* (New York: Holt, Rinehart and Winston, 1983).

POETRY

MARLAINA KREININ

INNER LIGHT

The climb is arduous,
A foothold gained,
Clinging to ancient rock,
Is lost. And gained again.

Building
On remembrance and promise,
Buoyed by sheer will
To surge upward.

Held steady by a primordial pull,
The eye focuses
On the imagined white light
Ahead.

A flash occurs,
A healing orgastic burst
Starting at the heartgut
Glowing into every extremity.

Revealing the light
Within
Enveloped in a sanctuary
Waiting to be entered.

The light expands
Filling up
More and more
The higher the reach.

It illuminates
The way,
Easing the dark corners,
Warming the ascent.

Other pilgrims
On their journey
See this beacon
And take heart.

POETRY

MARLAINA KREININ

WALKABOUT

An Aboriginal glued fast to work
Suddenly, without notice, unsticks,
Heeding the inner soaring buzz

An urgent overriding need to touch
Creation
Find images of origin
And be re-created once again.

The Bahai go walkabout
On the 19th day of every month,
Share reverence and celebration
Rekindle the luminous troth.

Sabbath day is a walkabout
For those who enter sacred time,
An oasis to dip into
And emerge anointed to light the week.

What is your walkabout?

What compelling energy bears you aloft
To hear the magnetic summoning bell,
To feel the touch of primal substance?

CONTRIBUTORS

Jude Aguwa is a theological anthropologist who until 1996 was a Senior Research Fellow at the Center for Igbo Studies, as well as a Senior Lecturer in the College of Education, at Abia State University, Uturu, Nigeria. Presently, Dr Aguwa teaches World Religions and the Sociology of Religion at Mercy College, Dobbs Ferry, New York. Dr. Aguwa's research interests include Christianity, African religions, and Indigenous Healing Systems. In keeping with his interdisciplinary approach to scholarship, he has edited important works on the political and agricultural traditions of the Igbo people of Nigeria.

M. Alejandro Chaoul is an Assistant Professor at the John P. McGovern Center for Health, Humanities and the Human Spirit, The University of Texas Medical School at Houston, and an Adjunct Assistant Professor at the Integrative Medicine Program at The University of Texas MD Anderson Cancer Center. He teaches in the areas of spirituality and health and integrative medicine. He is involved in research using Tibetan mind–body techniques with cancer patients and facilitates meditation for cancer patients and their support system, as well as for medical students, staff, and faculty. Dr. Chaoul's publications have focused on the role of mind–body practices in integrative cancer care and research, as well as Tibetan meditation and ritual practices within religious studies, humanities, and the intersection of humanities and medicine.

Lorenzo Cohen is Professor and Director of the Integrative Medicine Program at The University of Texas M.D. Anderson Cancer Center, Houston, Texas. Dr. Cohen is currently conducting clinical trials examining the biobehavioral effects of psychosocial interventions aimed at reducing the negative aspects of cancer treatment and improving quality of life (e.g., meditation, stress management, emotional writing, Hatha yoga, Tibetan yoga, tai chi/qigong, music therapy). He is interested in examining different types of complementary programs that can be easily incorporated into conventional treatment to decrease the psychophysiological sequelae associated with treatment. His research simultaneously assesses psychological, behavioral, and physiological factors in an attempt to better understand the cancer process.

Gary Dorrien is the Reinhold Niebuhr Professor of Social Ethics at Union Theological Seminary and Professor of Religion at Columbia University. His fourteen books include the recently completed trilogy, *The Making of American Liberal Theology*. His article in this issue is adapted from his forthcoming book, *Social Ethics in the Making: Interpreting an American Tradition* (Wiley-Blackwell).

Wakoh Shannon Hickey is an Assistant Professor of Religion at Alfred University in western New York. She earned a Ph.D. in Religion and Modernity at Duke University; her academic specialties are American religious history, Buddhism in the United States, and intersections between religion and medicine. She also completed a joint M.A./M.Div. at Pacific School of Religion, where she studied Buddhism and Christianity. She is ordained as a priest of Sōtō Zen, which she has practiced since 1983. Before taking her current academic post, she worked as a journalist, editor, and academic program manager, and as a chaplain in medical, psychiatric, and university settings.

Marlaina Kreinin, a visionary poet, honed her vision by the streams, rocks, and evergreen forests of Northern Michigan where she was raised. She holds an MS degree in Family Ecology and created a course entitled "A Holistic Approach to Family and Health," which she taught at Michigan State University. She is a co-author of a textbook, *Family Living*. For many years, as a professional storyteller, her favorite stories have centered on the environment, courage, and stretching our vistas.

Jim Perkinson is a long-time activist and educator from inner-city Detroit, currently teaching as Professor of Social Ethics at the Ecumenical Theological Seminary and lecturing in Inter-Cultural Communication Studies at the University of Oakland (Michigan). He holds a Ph.D. in theology/history of religions from the University of Chicago, is the author of *White Theology: Outing Supremacy in Modernity* and *Shamanism, Racism, and Hip-Hop Culture: Essays on White Supremacy and Black Subversion*; has written extensively in both academic and popular journals on questions of race, class, and colonialism in connection with religion and urban culture; and is a recognized artist on the spoken-word poetry scene in the inner city.

Bruce M. Sullivan is Professor of Religious Studies and Coordinator of the Asian Studies Program at Northern Arizona University, where he is also a Fellow of the Interdisciplinary Health Policy Institute. He has carried out ethnographic and literary research in India and teaches courses on Hindu and Buddhist religious traditions. He is the author of four books on aspects of the Hindu religious tradition and has published studies in the *Journal of the American Academy of Religion*, *Asian Theatre Journal*, and *Method & Theory in the Study of Religion*, among others.

Heidi Wayment is Professor of Psychology and a Fellow of the Interdisciplinary Health Policy Institute, Northern Arizona University. She edited and contributed to *Transcending Self-Interest: Psychological Explorations of the Quiet Ego* (American Psychological Assn., 2008). Her general interests are in social psychological issues related to self and identity and coping with negative life events. Her most recent research interests are concerned with understanding how individuals react to threat and loss and a general understanding of the bio-psycho-social-spiritual paths to a "quiet ego."

Bill Wiist is Special Assistant to the Executive Dean, College of Health & Human Services, Northern Arizona University. He is Senior Scientist in the Interdisciplinary Health Policy Institute, and Principal Investigator for Community Outreach for the Partnership for Native American Cancer Prevention, funded by a grant from the National Cancer Institute. He edited and contributed to *The Bottom Line or Public Health*, a book about the influence of corporations on health policy (Oxford University Press, 2010). His teaching specialization is the psychosocial theoretical foundations of public health, economic globalization and health, the relationship between spirituality/religion and health, and program planning and evaluation.

Emily Wu is a Ph.D. candidate in the Area of Cultural and Historical Studies of Religions at the Graduate Theological Union in Berkeley, California. She has recently defended her dissertation entitled "The Utilization of Spiritual Capital by the Practitioners of Traditional Chinese Medicine in the San Francisco Bay Area." Although not part of the dissertation, this article is derived from the ethnographic fieldwork conducted for it.

www.ingramcontent.com/pod-product-compliance
Lightning Source LLC
Chambersburg PA
CBHW040259170426
43193CB00020B/2948